HERE TO
LEAD

Mastering the Art of Leadership
in Order to Execute Strategy,
Advance Change, and
Drive Results

KELLY BARGABOS

HERE TO LEAD: Mastering the Art of Leadership
in Order to Execute Strategy, Advance Change,
and Drive Results

Copyright © 2022 by Kelly Bargabos

Printed in the United States of America

First paperback edition June 2022

Library of Congress Cataloging-in-Publication Data Control Number:
1-11359219671

ISBN 978-0-9994234-3-1 (paperback)
ISBN 978-0-9994234-4-8 (ebook)

Book cover and Interior design: GKS Creative
Edited by: Lisa Messinger and Melanie Zimmerman

www.kellybargabos.com

CONTENTS

A Note From the Author

Throughout my career, I've seen a serious gap between what it takes to become a good leader and what it takes to get things done. So many leaders appear to have it all on paper—the experience, the title, the fancy corner office—but can't seem to bring their leadership to life when it really matters.

With the benefit of experience, perspective and enough years behind me now to look back, take a breath and evaluate, I see clearly that there were a few defining moments in my career that stand out. The first occasion was when I was working in public accounting in order to earn my CPA. As an auditor for a regional firm, I had the opportunity to work on all aspects of the audit, from planning to testing to compiling the financial statements, and was also able to complete the tax return, which allowed me to see the entire engagement from start to finish. At one point, a few years in, the flow from transaction to general ledger account to financial statement suddenly made perfect sense. That ability to understand how all of it works together has never left me. I consider myself fortunate, as I've also realized throughout my career that this doesn't happen for everyone at the same rate, and sometimes it doesn't happen at all.

The second major revelation came about twenty years into my career. I had moved from a small operation where I was the CFO/COO to a larger office in a major city, suddenly a Vice President on a management committee of ten to twelve other executives and senior leaders. I distinctly remember a time when I looked around the table at my colleagues and realized that I was indeed capable, talented, intelligent and had earned my seat. I had spent my career with a deep desire to work hard, to do a good job, to become a good leader and I realized that I had achieved much of what I had so sincerely and earnestly desired. I settled into a new confidence that was both unexpected and rewarding.

It was during this period when I began to realize that being a good leader wasn't enough. This epiphany was the genesis for *Here to LEAD*. I loved this company and the work I did. But I noticed that as a leadership team, we spun our wheels... a lot. We talked about the same things over and over again. Every management meeting seemed to be regurgitating the same old status of stale projects. I began to watch and observe and seek to understand what was happening, and why. I worked with talented, smart, clever and motivated people. They challenged me all day, every day, to be better, to do better. It took everything for me to keep up with them. And yet, we still struggled to actually execute on projects, hit our deadlines and implement change. I became fascinated with the idea of finding the reasons we were struggling. I changed jobs and moved to a senior leadership role in another city, with another team of amazing and talented people and was surprised that we had the same struggles.

Within the pages of *Here to LEAD* is the real-life business case study generated from my experience. Regardless of where you are on the leadership spectrum—experienced or new, aspiring or accomplished—*Here to LEAD* is a resource or tool that you can keep in your office, on your desk, in your bag, or at home, that you can turn to over and over again for practical tools, insight and advice on how to bring your leadership to life on a daily basis. If you are a leader, there is no doubt that you are facing challenges, like leading staff through change, making quality decisions, or staying on track with strategy. It is my sincere hope that you will find the answers you need in this book.

Let's LEAD. It's what we're here for.

INTRODUCTION

There is a crack in everything. That's how the light gets in.
—LEONARD COHEN

It's fair to say that my father is the voice inside my head, most of the time. He is not only the king of dad jokes and puns, he also has a way of unloading wisdom in one-liners containing metaphors and analogies that generations today might not even understand. He'd say things like, "I'm busier than a one-armed paper hanger with an itch," or "That guy could screw up a two-car funeral." I've also heard him say, many times, that you only find out what you're really made of in times of crisis. "When the pressure's on and the heat is rising, that's when you see the cracks." My dad was referring to an engine, of course, but also people. Overheating and stressful operating conditions can cause cracks to develop in a car's cylinder head. When extremely damaged, it may start to vent exhaust directly into the engine space, which will then cause smoke to billow out from under the hood. Your cracked head will no longer be hidden from view. The smoke is a telltale sign that your car has been under enough heat and stress to cause cracks in the head.

And so it was with me. It was a period of intense heat and pressure that allowed me to see for myself these things that I will share in these pages. My crisis not only showed me where my cracks were, it allowed me to understand my strengths and what I was capable of. **It was a crisis that led me to understand what I believe about leadership.**

Six years ago, I found myself in the middle of an unexpected and sad divorce. We had been together for twenty-five years, so it took quite a bit of unraveling to separate our lives. A few months later, the company I worked for decided to close the office I had been based in for the previous ten years, near Syracuse, New York, and move the operation to their headquarters in Boston. I had an opportunity to take a new position with the same company and I took it. I figured it was a good chance to run away from the sadness that had settled in me and my empty house. I packed up and sold my dream home that I had lived in for the last twelve years and moved to a city where I didn't know anyone. So in a very short period of time, I experienced four of the top five life stressors—divorce, sale of a home, job change and a move to a new city. The heat was intense. I spent plenty of time listening to my playlist of sad songs while drinking wine and wallowing in typical mid-life crisis questions. Questions like, why am I here? Why did this happen to me? Who am I? What does it all mean?

I'm sure you have questions of your own right now, like, what does any of that have to do with leadership? Stay with me. I'll get there soon, I promise.

Just weeks before I left my hometown and moved to Boston, I began a romantic long-distance relationship. I hadn't been single in a very long time and was sure no one would ever find me attractive or love me again. I whined about it to my good friend, Craig, a guy I'd known in high school. We were both divorced after long marriages and had begun talking on the phone the summer after my ex-husband moved out. I confessed to him that I couldn't imagine kissing somebody new or getting naked in front of someone who hadn't known my twenty-one-year-old body with perkier breasts and a flatter stomach. I was convinced no one would find my middle-aged self interesting or desirable. Craig wasn't buying it. "Brush your teeth, put on deodorant, you'll be fine," he said.

He also told me he would never marry again. He didn't believe there was any reason for it if you didn't intend to have kids. I was horrified by his attitude. I liked being married. I wanted to grow old with someone. I don't know why, but it really bothered me that if I was lucky enough to find someone to be with for the rest of my life, it would likely be with someone who hadn't known me when I was young.

It was a surprise to both Craig and me when our friendship developed into something that gave my days a new design. When I woke up, I texted him "Good morning," and watched my phone and the clock until almost noon for his Pacific-coast-timed response. My day didn't begin until I'd heard from him. He was awake while I fell asleep and I found comfort in that. By October, I knew I had fallen in love. It took me until just before Christmas to tell him.

We texted the play-by-play details of our days and couldn't wait to see the other's face that night, thanks to FaceTime. We went on dates by finding movies that were simultaneously playing in our respective time zones and would each go to the theater alone. We'd text after we got our popcorn and found our seats and then turn our phones off while we watched the movie. Afterwards, we would call each other and talk about it for the rest of the night. We recorded television shows and movies at home and watched them together on our couches, three thousand miles apart. We shared love songs, books and bottles of wine. We shared our days and our nights and made love despite the distance.

The only problem with the relationship was that Craig lived in San Diego and I had just moved to Boston. We dated long distance for almost two years before we realized how hard it was to love someone on the opposite coast. Something had to change. Less than two years after I had divorced, changed jobs, sold my home and moved to a strange city, I moved again, across the country to another strange city, where this time I knew only one person.

I knew from my transition to Boston that to feel at home in a foreign place I needed to find a few things. It didn't take me too long after arriving in San Diego to find my closest CVS/Walgreens drug store and a grocery store that offered something to fill the hole left by Wegmans. I had a yellow sticky note in my wallet with instructions from Derek, my Boston hairdresser, on the color and brand he used to cover my grays and the technique to cut my curls so they had the least amount of frizz. I found my new favorite hairdresser on the first try. Only women will really understand how frightening it is to leave a hairdresser behind and be faced with finding a new one. It is even more daunting than dating again after a twenty-year marriage. It wasn't too long before I found a dentist that didn't try to upsell me, so I didn't have to worry about falling behind on my six-month cleanings. In my new strange city, these things anchored me in the familiar and settled me. I could exhale, and sleep at night once I knew where I could get toilet paper and mascara, almond milk and bananas, and get my hair and teeth done.

But I couldn't Yelp or Google map my way to a new job or a new professional network. The mid-life personal crisis I had been navigating had created a mid-career crisis and I was faced with starting over professionally.

Instead of a playlist of sad songs and wine, I had my resume in front of me and a cup of tea (and sometimes wine), but the questions were the same: Who am I professionally? What have I accomplished? What does it all mean? Why am I here?

I moved into a small condo near the beach for three months while Craig and I transitioned to a life together. I needed to figure out what I was going to do next. I hadn't been without a job since I had waitressed in high school. I certainly had never in my life quit a job without having another one lined up. My father had drummed into me that bit of career advice that so many of us have heard, that the best time to look for a job was when you have one. I had always agreed with him. Other than a week or two for vacations, I had never taken time off in my entire career. Finding myself unemployed and in a new city was unsettling, for my dad and for me.

Looking for a new job in my hometown would have been much easier. People knew me. I had a track record. I had a large network of family and friends, and friends of friends, and had former co-workers sprinkled throughout the city in different companies. I had left a company and position that I truly loved and was thriving in. I was Vice President of Finance for a diamond brand, and had recently been named Vice President of Operational Excellence.

INTRODUCTION

I did not have a professional network in San Diego. I was faced with having to sell myself to people who had no idea who I was or what I was capable of. I found out very quickly at my small kitchen table in Pacific Beach that I would need to answer those nagging questions if I was going to find my next job.

Who was I? It didn't take me too long to answer. I was a leader. Yes, that's it. I was a leader. But I couldn't help but wonder, so what? What kind of leader was I? That question took longer to answer and required some effort. I worked at defining what type of leader I had become throughout my career. But the questions kept coming, one leading to another. After I defined what type of leader I was, I still found myself asking, so what? Why should an organization hire me? What is it that I can do for them? What value do I add as this type of leader? And so I began the work of excavating and digging up and carving away until a form began to emerge.

My husband (yes, Craig changed his stance on marriage) is a talented and award-winning watercolor artist and is often asked to perform live demonstrations and workshops. I've watched him take a blank piece of paper and a photo of a scene that inspired him, and create a beautiful painting that moved people to tears. The first demo I attended, I was nervous for him. He stood in front of a large open room at a table that held his blank paper, palette, water, and all the other tools he needed. A camera was rigged above him, projecting everything he did onto a large screen in the front of the room.

Craig started the painting with broad strokes, using colors that I didn't see in the photo he was re-creating. It didn't look like anything recognizable at first. But he kept going. Eventually he added enough structure; the frame of the building, the outline of the street, a tree or two, so that the page had the promise of something. Midway through the demo, it still didn't look like much, and I was afraid he was going to run out of time. One hundred people were seated on the edge of their vinyl folding chairs, watching every move he made. What if he didn't pull it out? What if it didn't come together? Craig wasn't nervous at all. He understood his process. He knew where he was going and how to get there. Just as he was nearing the final stage, he brushed on a dark color that he hadn't used yet, and the audience gasped. Even his fellow artists were shocked he would be so bold, so fearless, or perhaps even foolish. "It's okay. You need the darks for the light to shine," Craig said, reassuring us that all was not lost.

Then, another stroke or two, a new color from the palette, some details added and as we watched, a beautiful image appeared. The audience and I breathed a sigh of relief and wonder. It wasn't just a re-creation of the photo. Craig had taken artistic license by changing colors and the position of the sun, he added people and omitted a tree that didn't work for his vision. He created a focal point and a path for the beholder to travel while viewing this piece of art. He transformed a static image, frozen in time and place, and gave it new life.

I was far enough along in my career when my crisis hit to know that I was a leader, but I had never gone through the process of defining what that meant to me. My static image of my career was my resume. I had a job as a fixed asset accountant lined up before I graduated from college at a company that leased computers to businesses. That was a real thing in the eighties. Two weeks after I started, the company filed for bankruptcy. A handful of the executives started their own business and I became a staff accountant at this startup company. It was a great experience but lasted less than a year before that company also folded. I was one year out of college and my career was already floundering. My boss at the startup referred me to a partner at a regional public accounting firm. My first day was less than two weeks later in January 1990 and I was instantly immersed in "busy season," working twelve-hour days and weekends, at a firm of all-male partners at a time when women were not allowed to wear pants! Seriously. Dresses and suits with skirts. I remember trudging around during winter in upstate New York, from one assignment to another, with my black audit bag and cold air blowing up my panty-hosed legs as I filled up my car with gas. I studied for the CPA exam and over the next five years passed all four parts and gained my certification. I took a job at a large, public, cooperative and over the next twelve years, moved among business units and positions following a traditional path of accountant/analyst, manager, and assistant controller, but eventually grew restless with accounting. I took an operations position with the heating oil and propane division after I convinced the CEO that I was the right person for the job. He was concerned that a woman wouldn't be able to earn the respect of the male truck drivers and technicians in the field. While I set about proving him wrong, I learned that I loved operations and began to develop my problem-solving skills.

The cooperative had a long history of financial difficulties and eventually filed bankruptcy and sold off divisions. After numerous restructuring plans, my position was eliminated. Six weeks later I was hired as CFO at a small diamond brand in Skaneateles, New York, that had recently been purchased by a large diamond brand out of Boston. A couple of years in, I became COO and was responsible for all aspects of the operation except for sales and marketing.

My resume and work experience was solid. I was a CPA with a finance and operations background, and had held a variety of positions in different industries. It looked good on paper. But again, it was a static image. I struggled with what it all meant and what I should do with it. I answered the who am I question, but why was I here?

I sat down with a blank piece of paper, and made some broad brushstrokes. What type of leader was I? It didn't look like much at first. One answer to a question begged another brushstroke. What was I good at? What did I like to do? Why should someone pay me to be a leader in their company? A structure began to take shape. But I had to keep working it. I had to go through the process before I could see the result of my work.

Here to LEAD is the completed portrait of the image I created through that soul-searching and question-answering process. This is what I've come to believe about myself, about leadership, and where our true power lies— using leadership to execute strategy, advance change and drive results.

Artists like Craig develop their confidence by continual study and practice. Whether it is playing the piano or guitar, painting, writing, acting or singing, any artist will tell you that the only way to develop and master your craft is to do it, as frequently and as consistently as you can. Artists must work on their craft and leadership is no different. It is an art that we practice and perfect over the lifetime of our careers.

In the pages that follow, we will discover the art of Authentic Leadership that will allow you to execute strategy, advance change and drive results and ultimately transform your leadership from a static image on paper to a powerful force.

It's when the heat rises that we find out what we're made of. Cracks may be the result of heat and stress, but the cracks also let the light in. My professional crisis let me see who I really was and what I was capable of as a leader. My hope is that you can use what I've learned and discover what you know and believe about leadership for yourself, without having to go through a crisis.

Let's **LEAD**. It's what we're here for.

What to Expect in This Book

LEAD is an acronym that will provide an ANCHOR as you move through the lessons contained in these pages. Each section begins with a relevant quote followed by chapters that further explore the topic. Chapters examine various problems and challenges that leaders face and suggest solutions that will help you overcome the obstacle. Each chapter includes these elements:

 ANCHORS provide the four main sections of *Here to LEAD*.
1. Leadership
2. Execute Strategy
3. Advance Change
4. Drive Results

 GUARDRAILS keep you from going off a cliff, or veering over the center line in the road into a head-on collision. In this context, guardrails are real-life practical tools that will help you in your day-to-day leadership and keep you centered on the right path.

 TRUTH BOMBS will challenge and provoke you.

 TIME IN THE SEAT exercises are for you to practice your craft of leadership.

 HEADLINES summarize the most important things for you to remember.

PART ONE

LEADERSHIP

*Leadership is seeing the possibilities in
a situation while others are seeing the limitations.*

—JOHN C. MAXWELL

CHAPTER ONE

LEADERSHIP IS _____

WHAT IS LEADERSHIP?

There are as many answers to this question as there are books written about this topic. The truth is, there are many definitions. Sure, they have some common elements and attributes, but at the end of the day, how you define leadership is always personal. I developed my own definition many years ago while participating in an intense yearlong leadership program. It is clearly not the only definition, nor is it the best articulated, but it hits on the key points. I check in with it periodically, and fifteen years later, it still resonates with me.

Leadership is the ability to influence diverse people or situations with integrity, charisma, vision and passion. True leaders are servants of the people they lead and the vision that inspires them.

I explained in the introduction that this wasn't going to be a book about becoming a leader, but instead it is about how to leverage and use our leadership in the most effective way. In order to anchor us in this topic and provide framework for the rest of the material, we'll spend the first two chapters discussing the meaning of leadership, specifically defining what it means to us personally.

HOW DO YOU DEFINE LEADERSHIP?

Take a few minutes and think about what leadership means to you and develop your own definition. It can be one word, a sentence or two, or a paragraph. It may be a quote from a leader you most admire, or from your favorite leadership book. You don't have to write your own; it is perfectly okay to use someone else's. I've shared my definition; now take some time and think about yours. Or, if you're not ready yet, tag this page and come back to it later and fill in the blank.

Leadership is _____.

To help you get started, here are a few more of my favorites.

"A leader is one who knows the way, goes the way, and shows the way."

—JOHN C. MAXWELL

"A leader is anyone who takes responsibility for finding the potential in people and processes, and who has the courage to develop that potential."

—BRENÉ BROWN

"A good leader inspires people to have confidence in the leader, a great leader inspires people to have confidence in themselves."

—ELEANOR ROOSEVELT

"A genuine leader is not a searcher for consensus, but a molder of consensus."

—MARTIN LUTHER KING JR.

WHAT DOES IT TAKE TO BECOME A LEADER?

There are many answers to this question, many books written about how to become a leader, and countless theories, formulas and personality tests. For me, true leaders have three traits in common. Leaders:

1. **Aspire.**
2. **Study.**
3. **Practice.**

1. Aspire

In order to become a leader, you first have to have the desire or aspiration. You have an internal desire to lead people, projects or initiatives. Not everyone does, and that's okay. How do you know if you have an aspiration to leadership?

It comes naturally. You were probably the captain of your soccer or football team, or elected to student council. In college, when you were assigned the dreaded team project, you assumed the role of leader because it made you uneasy and irritated when everyone else on the team stared blankly at each other or their phones, or discussed their favorite pizza toppings instead of getting done what your team was tasked to do.

The absence of leadership bothers you. More than anything, a lack of leadership drives me crazy. I can't stand to be part of something—whether it's a sports team, a company, a volunteer organization, or a family dinner for twenty-five—that lacks leadership. We need it. Without it, people flounder and wander aimlessly. There have been many times when I avoided joining situations because I witnessed a lack of leadership and knew that if I joined, I was, for all intents and purposes, signing up to lead it. My family has called me bossy once or twice. But I prefer to believe I have strong leadership skills. I know if the hamburger buns are to the right of the meat platter and the condiments are to the left, you will have complete chaos in the buffet line that will bring the entire operation to a halt. Don't get me started on the placement of plates and utensils.

Leaders provide vision. There is a Bible verse (Proverbs 29:18) that says without vision the people perish. Whether or not you believe in the Bible doesn't matter. If you aspire to leadership, this is a valid truth.

You enjoy the satisfaction of helping a team accomplish their goal. If you aspire to leadership, you derive great satisfaction from watching your teams accomplish what they set out to do. As a leader, one of my most important jobs is to make sure that the people I'm responsible for have what they need to be successful. This is where a lot of people miss the mark. Often, ego is the motivation and the so-called leader is just looking to be the hero. According to my definition, this is not true leadership. "True leaders are servants of the people they lead and the vision that inspires them."

If any of the above scenarios sound familiar, most likely you do aspire to become a leader. Not everyone feels this. My father had a saying that so-and-so "couldn't lead themselves out of a paper bag." It may sound a little cruel, but the truth is, there are many kinds of people: Some are leaders and others are happy to let others lead. They are driven to work hard and contribute, and are talented, necessary members of the team, but not leaders.

2. Study

Becoming a good leader involves study. There is an abundance of resources available to us from leadership gurus and other experts who have written books on this topic. Obviously, if you picked up this book, you are interested in leadership. If you haven't yet studied the subject, find some books that resonate with you and search out leadership conferences and seminars. Ask your company for leadership training. If they offer it, sign up for it. I have been fortunate in my career to have worked for organizations that were willing to invest in my leadership development. I've studied leadership at Syracuse University, Suffolk University in Boston, and completed a yearlong community program called *Leadership Greater Syracuse*. I've been to plenty of conferences and seminars and love to read and listen to leadership experts. **Leadership takes study**.

I studied to become an accountant, first in college and then on my own to pass the CPA exam. I bought review guides that were four inches thick and committed myself to a hand-painted desk shoved in a corner of my bedroom every night after work. My study has been ongoing throughout my career to keep up with continuous learning. My sister is an attorney, which required law school and then studying to pass the bar exam. My other sister is an RN, which required nursing school and further study to pass her licensing test. My father decided to make a career change at fifty years old and became a minister. He didn't attend Bible school, but he studied relentlessly by taking classes, becoming an apprentice and sitting under great ministers, and reading everything he could get his hands on.

If it is truly important to you and a priority, you will find the time and the resources that work for you. Invest in your leadership with study.

3. Practice

Finally, aspiring and studying will only take you so far. **You need time in the seat.** When my eighteen-year-old stepson got his driver's license, the circumstances were very different from when I got mine. I grew up in a rural community and from the age of twelve on, I rode three-wheelers (before quads there were three-wheelers), snowmobiles, and the tractor lawn mower on a weekly basis, happy to get a tan while mowing the lawn.

My older sister taught me to drive a car and gave me time in the seat before I was old enough to get my permit. When I was fifteen and aspiring to drive, she was sixteen and already fully licensed. On the weekends when we were headed into town for a night out, she would take the long way, turning off Route 13 onto Bones Road. Bones Road was a narrow country road without any white lines before the ditch, or any yellow markings down the middle, and it was rare to encounter another car. My sister pulled our car over as soon as we turned off the main road so that we could switch seats in the Chevy Chevette, which was a standard, or manual transmission. I would get to drive for three whole miles before we'd switch seats again, just before we hit Route 69. By the time I turned sixteen, getting my license was just a formality. I could already drive a car or pickup truck with an automatic or manual transmission, stick on the floor or column. I still studied and completed a driver's education course and practiced whenever my parents or older brother and sister would let me have the keys, but the learning curve was definitely less than it was for my stepson Garrett.

Garrett hadn't been behind the wheel before. It was scary getting into the car with him the first time. I sat in the back seat, fully buckled in and burrowed in the corner, praying, and looking for my safe space, mentally and physically. His father and I took him to a church parking lot nearby so others wouldn't be at risk from a driver with no experience. As my husband started to patiently talk him through driving around the parking lot, and Garrett pulled into and then backed out of spaces, we noticed a few cars pulling in. It was a Saturday, so we had assumed a church lot was a good option. But in the span of five minutes, at least twenty or thirty cars pulled into the lot. We surmised either a funeral or a wedding was about to take place so we knew the lesson would be cut short. Craig walked him through parking one last time so he could take over and get us out of there.

"Okay, now turn your wheel to the right and just coast into the space between the white lines," Craig said.

"Good. Now when you're all the way in, press the brake in gently to stop."

Garrett stepped on the gas instead of the brake, careening us forward toward a large oak tree that none of us had noticed until we were suddenly aiming right for it at a frighteningly high speed.

"No, the brake, the brake! Holy shit! Stop!" Craig said.

Lucky for all of us, Garrett found the brake just in time and we all jerked forward and back as he found the right pedal and jammed it down.

"Put the car in park," Craig said, and we all took a deep breath and exhaled slowly as we realized we had narrowly avoided a collision with the tree.

We then did the responsible thing and bought Garrett driving lessons, which started at the beginning and taught him everything he needed to know about driving a car, along with the rules of the road, and he made great strides. In other words, he *aspired* to drive and *studied* appropriately.

But I knew that the only thing that would get him to a point where he didn't have to think about the gas or the brake pedal was time in the seat. He could aspire to drive, study the handbook to pass the test, even pass the driver's test and obtain his license, but the only way he was going to become a good driver was *practice*. **He needed time in the seat.** This is the only thing that would transform his book knowledge into practical skills that would allow him to confidently change lanes on the 8 freeway, park between the lines on the first try, or safely back out of our driveway on the curved hilltop that is loaded with blind spots.

The more a painter paints or a writer writes or a musician plays, the better they will become at their art. **Just like any other craft, to grow and develop as a leader, you need time in the seat, which will solidify everything you've learned and studied, and will also allow you to find out what works, what doesn't work and what you need to change.**

How do you find opportunities to practice leadership? Apply for leadership positions. If you've never led a team of people, look for an opportunity to lead a project or initiative. It's not just the big titles or promotions that will give you time in the seat. Start small, but start. Get in the seat. A key element of this book are exercises that will allow you to get in the seat and practice your leadership skills.

Your Turn In The Seat

1. Do you ASPIRE to leadership? Take a moment and think back over your life, beginning with your earliest memories, through school, college, sports, etc. Write down some examples where leadership roles came naturally to you.

2. Have you STUDIED leadership? Take a moment and write down the books you've read, the courses you've taken, where you've studied. If you haven't yet, do some research and develop goals to study leadership this year.

3. Have you PRACTICED leadership yet? What time in the seat have you had? Have you led a project? Have you led a team of direct reports? If not, develop goals to start small. What project could you volunteer to lead? Is there a charitable organization that you can volunteer for and lead a team? Is there an open supervisory or management position that you've had your eye on?

CHAPTER TWO

WHAT DOES LEADERSHIP MEAN TO YOU?

THE ELEVATOR PITCH OF LEADERSHIP

An elevator pitch can be relevant in many situations or applications. As a writer, for every book, novel, play, or project I've written, I've developed a two to three sentence summary that I can rattle off to anyone who asks the fated question, "What's your book about?" or "What do you write about?"

This type of summary is dubbed the elevator pitch, based on the premise that you need to be able to articulate your idea, your project, yourself, whatever it is you're selling, in the few minutes you have while riding in an elevator with someone you've been dying to get in front of. I don't think I've ever rattled off one of these in an actual elevator, but I have used the concept at a party, at the dinner table, at a job interview or a pitch session at a writer's conference. We all have those moments when we are put on the spot and asked a question. Rather than fumbling through words and rambling on, and then walking away kicking yourself for sounding like a bumbling idiot, having a practiced pitch you can share with anyone will not only impress whomever you're addressing, it will give you the confidence to actually seek out those key people, hoping they'll ask the tough question, rather than hide in the corner and pray no one talks to you.

At the time of my mid-professional life crisis, I had developed several elevator pitches for different creative projects I was working on, but I had never done one professionally. Before I could summarize my career aspirations in the few sentences of a true elevator pitch, I realized that I had to work through three questions. This exercise allowed me to get to the point where I could articulate how I view myself, what I do and how I want others to see me.

1. **What type of leader am I?**
2. **What do I like to do?**
3. **What will others say about how I lead?**

1. What type of leader am I?

I began by making a list of all the leaders I'd known in my life and career and what I learned from them. I've learned from every position I've held and every leader I've worked for—the good, the bad and the ugly. Understanding how I *didn't* want to lead helped me figure out the kind of leader I wanted to be. This exercise was hard at first. When I sat and tried to make a list of the good leaders I'd known, I couldn't come up with a single one. Then I tried to think about my earliest leaders. Again, nothing came to me. But I didn't give up and dug deep. I started with those who had had positional leadership in my life. My dad, my coach and my pastor.

My father was a foreman at a gravel pit for more than twenty years. He taught me that leaders work hard and side by side with their team, willing to do whatever was necessary. He gave me my work ethic and the practical aspect of my leadership. "Any job worth doing, is worth doing well," he would say many, many times throughout my life, and it is his voice I hear in my head whenever I'm tempted to take a shortcut.

My father never asked his employees to do anything he wasn't willing to do himself. He left the house every morning between four-thirty and five a.m., black lunchbox in hand. It didn't matter what we had going on the night before, he got up every day at the same time. He took me and my two sisters to work with him long before *Take Your Daughters to Work Day* or *Girl*

Dad was a thing. Besides sitting in the trailer eating butterscotch candies with Remy, the guy who weighed the trucks as they left the gravel pit and took the tickets so he could bill the customers, we also had a front-row seat in the dump trucks and loaders, next to my dad or his workers.

My father worked alongside his crew, and for the extremely risky and scary jobs, he would send himself. At the gravel pit was a crusher that shattered large stones and rocks into #1 or #2 stone, as they're known in that industry. Occasionally, the chute would get plugged and the only way to unplug it would be to send somebody down the conveyer belt. My dad didn't send the smallest or youngest guy. He didn't send the new guy or the one nobody liked. He shimmied himself down a forty-foot conveyer belt on his back holding a hammer and chisel. There wasn't enough room to sit up or move your feet when you got to the bottom. After he hammered and chiseled into pieces the stone that had been causing the problem, he shimmied back up the belt. He said it was like crawling through a pipe on your back, and you couldn't let your mind wander or you might become claustrophobic and panic very quickly. He had one of the guys stand close by in case he got stuck and needed to be pulled out with a rope, and also to make sure nobody turned the crusher on while he was in there.

My dad drove the dump truck, ran the bulldozer and led his men while working side by side with them. He was the OG of the "roll your sleeves up" leader. In business today, we use phrases like, "this is a hands-on" role or a "roll your sleeves up" position, to make sure people know we expect them to work. **I will be forever grateful to my dad for his work ethic and practical, get-it-done mentality that transferred to me.**

When I think back as early as I can remember, the first leader that comes to mind, other than my dad, is my field hockey coach from high school. I respected my coach without question. She cared about each one of us personally, but that didn't stop her from kicking our butts during practice and expecting us to not just show up, but to show up ready to play.

Before my junior year of high school ended for the summer, Coach let the team know that she expected us to show up in August in shape and ready to play at our first practice. She knew that if we were already conditioned, she wouldn't have to waste time on cardio and strength training, and could instead get right to the business of skills, which is where we would win or lose a game. Along with her expectations, she gave us the plan to get there in a stapled packet of purple-inked ditto copy pages. So that summer between my junior and senior years, I woke up at 6 a.m., before I had to report to my job at the restaurant, and ran three miles, jumped over my hockey stick one hundred times, completed one hundred sit-ups, dribbled around my backyard dodging flower beds and lawn furniture, practiced stick skills, and did everything else on her list.

In August, when practice began, I showed up in the best shape of my life. Coach recognized it and started me every game. I won MVP that year and was on the All-Star team. I'm not sure I appreciated or realized what she was doing, but I know now that she gave us her expectations, a plan to get there, held us accountable to it, and then rewarded us with playing time on the field.

My coach also wasn't afraid to fail or be vulnerable. Once, in the final minute of a game with one of our biggest rivals, Canastota, I failed to stop a ball on a corner shot. Coach yelled and screamed with hands waving and spit flying on the sidelines, "Bargabos! What is the matter with you???"

I was devastated by her frustration and disappointment with me. I was already embarrassed by the flubbed shot, and her reaction killed me. But life went on. To be honest, I don't remember if we won that game or not, but I remember what she did next. At the end of the season, she gave me a thank-you card. In the card she explained how that day on the field in Canastota had been a life lesson for her and changed her whole philosophy of coaching. After she yelled at me and was afraid she had destroyed my love for the game and my respect for her, she realized that playing the game was about so much more than just winning, and she wanted me to know that. Her ability and willingness to be a vulnerable leader and admit to a mistake that drove to a change in her coaching philosophy taught me that it was okay to be a strong, respected leader, and when you make a mistake, you apologize, say you were wrong, ask for forgiveness, and move on. **She taught me that true leaders are okay with vulnerability.** The lessons I learned on the hockey field are still with me today.

My pastor was another early leader who taught me about **vision and discipleship.** He demanded excellence from everyone—staff and volunteers—and developed a program that transformed interested members into disciples and leaders. In my twenties, I completed a twelve-week discipleship program that culminated in a heart-inspiring speech mirroring the one where Jesus pumped up his disciples to carry on the work after he left this world. The lessons from that program moved me then and have stayed with me through the years.

These earliest leaders of mine, before I entered the professional world, modeled a leadership that was hands-on and practical, vulnerable and authentic, rooted in vision and discipleship.

Of course, in my more than twenty-five years in the business world, I've worked for all kinds of leaders—good and bad, toxic and visionary, effective and useless. Most leaders don't fit neatly into one label, but instead can possess all of these traits depending on the situation. I am grateful for every leader I've worked for, because they've all made me the leader I am today.

When I began this exercise of defining what kind of leader I was, I began by listing the type of leaders I had experienced and what I remembered about them. Unfortunately, a common theme developed around what I had witnessed that I knew I didn't want to replicate in my own leadership.

Mistakes I've seen other leaders make:
- Afraid to fail—therefore afraid to make decisions.
- Paralysis by analysis—trying to get the analysis 100% right when 80% is good enough to make the decision.
- Communication extremes—thinking that communication means you tell everyone everything all the time, or else not valuing communication at all.
- Treating people unkindly or disrespectfully.

- Not holding people accountable, including themselves and senior leaders.
- Keeping weak or toxic people on a team too long.
- Unable to maintain focus.
- Trying to implement too many things at once, making lasting change elusive.
- Lack of vision for the organization or not effectively communicating their vision throughout the organization.

Articulating these things helped me figure out the kind of leader I wanted to be and answer that first question, what type of leader am I?

2. What do I like to do?

To answer this question, I spent some time looking over my resume and career history and thinking about the positions I had held, the projects I had worked on, and what stood out to me. Whenever I prepped for a job interview, I made sure I had examples and talking points of successful projects and career highlights. I looked at these notes and looked for common themes.

3. What will others say about how I lead?

Again, to answer this question I thought about the leaders I had witnessed throughout my life, and what I had responded to. How did I like to be led? How would I want to be treated, corrected or rewarded? During one of my leadership programs, we were tasked with writing a personal mission statement. I wrote the following very early in my life and career:

I will use my skills and abilities to bring information, truth, justice and inspiration into my world and all those around me. My work will have an impact, cause change, improve things and combat negative forces or trends. I will help those in need. I will build where there was nothing. I believe that anyone and everyone can change, and that each new day is a chance to turn it all around.

Guardrail

The full exercise that I took myself through is below.

1. What type of leader am I?

- ✓ Authentic: I am honest, committed, flawed, curious and open. Authentic leadership is also self-aware, not ruled by fear, comfortable with making mistakes, and able to make the tough decisions while remaining vulnerable and transparent.
- ✓ Collaborative: I believe in building strong teams with accountability. I am also able to rely on the expertise of others. I don't need to be the one with all the answers, I just need to be able to find them or the people who have them.
- ✓ Capable: I possess business acumen, am hardworking, focused and educated.
- ✓ Strong: I am decisive, accountable and willing to make the tough decisions.

2. What do I like to do?

- ✓ Find solutions.
- ✓ Problem-solve: When someone tells me about a problem or challenge, my brain immediately shifts into problem-solving mode.
- ✓ Reverse trends.
- ✓ Implement change.
- ✓ Maximize productivity.

3. What will others say about how I lead?

How I treat people is important to me. I never want to make someone feel bad, or shamed, or less than. I'm not interested in finger-pointing. When something goes wrong, or mistakes are made, I'm less interested in who is responsible and more interested in what happened that led to this result and how we avoid it in the future.

I want to lead with:

- ✓ Kindness and respect.
- ✓ Open and consistent communication: This doesn't mean you have to tell everyone everything. Circumstances do not always allow for that. Be transparent when you can, honest when you can't, but most importantly, be consistent.
- ✓ Accountability and operational excellence.

Important Note: This is not <u>the</u> list. It is <u>a</u> list. Your list and answers to those three questions will be different. I'm not suggesting that what leadership looks like for me should be the same for you. Using the answers to the three questions above, I was able to consolidate and formulate the pitch below.

My elevator pitch:

I am an authentic, collaborative, capable leader with a passion for finding solutions, reversing negative trends, maximizing productivity and implementing change. I am committed to leading with kindness, respect, and open and consistent communication, while holding myself and others accountable for Operational Excellence.

Your Turn In The Seat

Warm up:

Make a list below of all the leaders who have influenced you, good and bad. Next to their name, write three words that describe their leadership style. Next, write what they did on a daily basis that made an impression on you, whether positive or negative. What did you see them do well? What mistakes did they make? Finally, what was their reputation? What did people say about them? Remember, the point of these three questions is to develop a summary statement, or elevator pitch, that can let someone know in a short time who you are, what you are good at, and how you do it.

Leader	Style	Daily Impressions	Reputation
Mr. Grant	Old-school. Fair. Strong.	Knew what he wanted and how to ask his team for it. Held people accountable. Wasn't open to new ideas, thought he always knew best.	Tough, impatient, honest.
Michael Scott	Isolated. Arrogant. Motivated.	Unqualified for the position, but trying to do his best. Good intentions but also offensive and tone deaf.	Genuine, honest, clueless.

1. What type of <u>leader</u> am I, or do I aspire to be? Hint: Scan the warm-up exercise you just completed. What stands out? If you need help, consult the list of leadership attributes below and circle any that resonate with you. Write down at least three, but no more than five.

   Some leadership attributes:

Commanding	Capable	Inspirational
Collaborative	Authentic	Communicative
Strong	Intellectual	Passionate
Entrepreneurial	Creative	Empowering
Brave	Committed	Innovative
Honest	Confident	Enlightened

2. What do I like to <u>do</u>? Hint: Look over your resume or accomplishments. What makes you feel proudest? What part of your day do you enjoy most?

3. What will others say about <u>how</u> I lead? Hint: What qualities as a human being are important to you? What qualities do you respond well to in others?

4. Summarize your answers in one or two clear and concise sentences. Memorize it! Hint: You are simply answering the questions of who you are, what you like to do, and how you do it.

You now have your very own elevator pitch. Well done. This is important work. Practice your summary out loud until you memorize it. Let it become your mantra. Don't let yourself get hung up if you don't feel like you're there yet. You may want to revisit this periodically and make adjustments as you grow and develop.

The truth is, leadership is an art that you will practice and perfect over your entire lifetime.

These questions and exercises are critical to understanding who you are as a leader and what leadership means to you. It helped me to answer the question of "Who am I?" But I still had no clue about what it all meant and why I was here. It felt good. Sounded good. Looked good on paper, but what did it all mean? Why would anyone hire me? In other words, **SO WHAT?**

CHAPTER THREE

THE FATE OF THE FANCY LIVING ROOM

I've had a friend since college who I'll call Jan. Jan was always more interested in appearances than I was. For example, on Sunday mornings at school, when most of us rolled out of bed and showed up at the dining room in sweatpants and ponytails, just in time before they shut down the bagel and cream cheese station, Jan would walk in with her clean hair in perfectly scrunched curls, eye shadow and mascara in place, wearing acid-washed jeans and a Benetton sweatshirt. She cared how she looked all the time. She also couldn't wait to get her own home someday. She knew exactly what she wanted.

A decade or so after college, Jan and her husband and four kids bought their dream house. It was a lovely four-bedroom colonial on a cul-de-sac in a quiet neighborhood. When you walked in the front door, the family room on the right was where the family spent most of their time watching television, eating meals, playing games and doing homework, and this room led into the den and the kitchen. The stairs were straight ahead and took you up to the bedrooms.

On the left side of the front door was the fancy living room. This room was off limits. No one was allowed to enter. Not the kids, the dogs, her husband or her friends, including me. This room was stunning, with pale gray carpet, a sofa and chair with a flowered pattern in soft colors, and a large formal dining room table that was always fully set with linens, china, silver, water goblets and wine glasses, and a centerpiece that changed with the seasons. The room was always photo-shoot ready, just like Jan in the college dining room, as if *Town and Country* might show up at any moment.

Jan was so intent on maintaining a perfect image in this room that every night before bed, she would vacuum the carpet that hadn't been used by anyone. She started at the far end by the kitchen and finished just at the entrance to the foyer. She could finish the job, turn out the light and walk up the stairs to bed without having to step on the carpet and leave footprints. She loved to go to bed and wake up to the lines in the plush carpet left behind by the vacuum cleaner.

I never really understood the point to all of this. Jan and her husband spent hundreds of thousands of dollars on this home. They spent thousands more on decorating this fancy room, and even called it a "living" room, but no one could enjoy it or live in it. It sat empty and idle. To me, it was a waste of money and space. Why have all those beautiful things if no one is allowed to enjoy them or to experience the benefits of them?

I've seen people and worked with people who treat their leadership the same way Jan treated this room. They invest time and money in becoming a good leader and acquiring the skills they need to be successful. They attend seminars, read all the books, take classes, pursue and attain positions with the right titles. They've got it all on paper. It looks good. But their leadership is wasted because they are not effectively using it on a daily basis, or allowing their teams and organizations to benefit from it.

Being a leader is more than the position you hold, the title you have, the degree you've earned, the money you make or the size of the company, department or team that you manage. Being a leader is much more than appearances, fancy corner offices or impressive titles and salaries. Being a leader is only useful, practical and meaningful when it is used in the daily practice of getting stuff done. Moving people forward. Creating change.

Building where there was nothing. Living rooms are meant to be lived in, to be used, to get dirty. So is leadership. **Leadership is meant to be used.**

The following chapters will teach you how to leverage your leadership for effectiveness and power, and to avoid the fate of the fancy living room.

LEAD. It's what we're here for.

Headlines

✓ Leaders ASPIRE.

✓ Leaders STUDY.

✓ Leaders PRACTICE.

✓ The ability to summarize who you are as a leader and what it means to you is a powerful exercise. Develop your own Elevator Pitch of Leadership.

✓ Leadership is meant to be used...avoid the fate of the fancy living room.

CHAPTER FOUR

BONUS—HOW TO INTERVIEW TO GET THE OFFER

Interviewing is like dating. Nobody loves it, but it is a necessary process if we're ever going to find "The One." It can also be an intimidating and overwhelming endeavor. When I was in the middle of my mid-career crisis, starting over in a city where I didn't know anyone, and trying to build a professional network from scratch, I met Megan Ahn, Founder and President of Accountants Direct, LLC Executive Search Firm. She was my first professional colleague in San Diego. I had gone to one of those networking events where I had high hopes of meeting people and making connections, but instead, most seemed to have already formed groups and cliques and wouldn't offer me a seat at their lunch table. It was fifth grade all over again.

I walked around trying to appear self-assured and like it was cool to be there alone, until I found the booth of a recruiting firm. That particular agency wasn't able to help me, but they gave me a list of three other recruiting firms to try in San Diego. Megan Ahn was on that list. When she returned my call a few days later, we hit it off right away. I loved her practical approach, her insight and her experience. Also, she was very well connected in San Diego and seemed to know everything about everyone in the area.

She became extremely valuable to me at a very challenging time in my life and career. Her insight and expertise into the interview process, along with practical tools and advice, helped me and they will help you, too.

Accountants Direct is a permanent placement business that places accounting and finance professionals in San Diego. Megan founded the company in 2002, and her goal has always been to find her accounting candidates their forever homes and to find her clients phenomenal short- and long-term healthy fits for their companies.

Here to LEAD is for leaders who are at all different levels and phases of their career. In the first few chapters, we learned how to define who we are as a leader and how to sell ourselves to anyone we encounter as we talk about who we are, what we like to do and what we're good at. When we begin our careers and are interviewing for positions, we're still gathering many different kinds of skills, and we're not really assessing much more than opportunity. But as we continue to grow and develop experience along with leadership, we begin to accumulate valuable tools in our toolbox. When we are interviewing, we want to have the ability to assess a good management team and a healthy company, and whether or not the opportunity is a match for our own skills and passion. We constantly change and develop as our career grows.

When I was looking for my next opportunity in San Diego and was preparing for an interview, Megan coached me. I sat in her office, pen in hand, leaning forward to make sure I didn't miss anything, as she shared her interview advice. Even though I had years of experience, and considered myself an accomplished and veteran interviewer, I had never received guidance and counsel that was as succinct, useful and practical.

Megan shared a story with me that applies to anybody who is interviewing, at any level, with any company, at any time. Here's the story she told me that day:

"Imagine you're out taking a walk, and you trip, and you twist your ankle. You make it home, put your ankle up, take a bunch of Advil or Tylenol and put some ice on it, and you think you're going to be just fine. An hour later, your ankle is so swollen and you're in so much pain that now you think not only is your ankle broken but your foot might even be broken. So you have a friend or significant other take you to the urgent care doctor. By the time you get to urgent care, you cannot even put weight on your foot. You just sit there crying. Your name is finally called and you limp into the doctor's office. You sit there in that little room, and then hear the knock on the door. The doctor walks in and asks you half a dozen questions. We've all been there. 'Have you ever broken your foot or your ankle before? Are you allergic to any medicine?' Then they examine you. They tell you they're going to take a peek and then send you for x-rays. If it's just a sprain, you'll come back, they'll give you some anti-inflammatories, and they'll wrap you up, give you some crutches, and send you home. But if it's bad, you're going to see an orthopedic surgeon. The urgent care doctor cannot help you.

"Here's the analogy to interviewing. When the urgent care doctor knocks on the door and enters the room, they know that the person inside that room is in pain. People do not show up to urgent care because they feel fine and they have nothing better to do. So when the urgent care doctor walks through that door, they know there's pain on the other side. Now, the urgent care doctor has years of experience. They can help you if you're having a heart attack, have the flu, if you cut your finger or had a surfing accident. Whatever it is, they can probably offer you some assistance. **But they only share the knowledge and expertise they possess that is relevant to your individual health crisis in that moment.** So they ask you some questions, and you tell them the answers, and then they decide if they can help you or not. When you need urgent care, you don't have time to find out where the urgent care doctor went to school or if they ever helped anybody with a broken or sprained ankle before.

"When you go to an interview, your mission is to walk through the door understanding that if this company is hiring, and they've read your resume and called you in, they have pain. People don't sit around reviewing a stack of resumes and calling people to ask them to come in because they have nothing better to do. They have pain and something on your resume piqued their interest, so when you walk through the door, put your urgent care hat on. **Listen and ask good questions** so that you can learn what their needs are and then begin to share your knowledge and expertise that is relevant to their pain.

"Your goal is to find out as much as you can about the opportunity, just like that urgent care doctor, so that you can identify if the job is a good fit for you. Is the work they need accomplished what you want on your resume, and is it an opportunity that will use your valuable skills and where you will continue to grow professionally in leadership and technical capabilities? At some point in your career, your technical skills become solid. Then it becomes about leadership and about surrounding yourself with people and projects that inspire, impassion, and motivate you moving forward. Then you can decide whether or not you liked the parking lot, or the location, or the receptionist enough to spend every day there."

That day in Megan's office, her urgent care story made sense to me and helped me frame everything I knew about interviewing in a new way. I've since used her advice many times and have shared these key takeaways with my friends and family whenever I get the chance.

1. Companies hire people they believe understand their pain and can help them resolve it, not people who try to tell them everything about themselves in an hour.

You have already proven you can work in different environments, different size companies and under different leadership types. You are highly educated, have a track record of work experience and, at this point in your professional career, there is no need to "sell." The best interviews are those in which information is exchanged, and the one to be sharing the most information initially should be the company in pain. They are in need, and as a candidate it is much more important for you to discover as much as possible about their pain, because this information makes it easy for you to know what information from your background is valuable to share. Think of the urgent care doctor, who only shares their knowledge and expertise that is relevant to a patient's pain. Empathetic doctors are good listeners, and once they understand the trouble, they offer their relevant knowledge and expertise. When the exchange of facts is specific and healthy, you will have the information you need to decide if the opportunity is a good fit for you.

2. The key to great interviewing is to always remember that it is not about you, no matter how much you wish it was.
When a company is interviewing a candidate with your level of experience and education, they have pain. They do not clear their calendar to interview for any other reason than they have pain that needs to be addressed. It is about them, not you.

3. It is your job to focus on their pain and then share what knowledge and expertise you have that is relevant.
The more you learn about their pain, the easier it will be for you to share what experience you have that is relevant and to determine if the job is a good fit for you professionally. Ask questions. Companies extend offers to candidates who they believe understand and can solve their pain. Your job is to keep moving forward if you are interested and ultimately have the company generate an offer, then you can decide if you want to say yes, no or make a counteroffer.

4. If a question comes up that you do not have direct or recent experience with, how you answer is important.
For example, "It seems you don't have experience in our industry?" Remember, they knew this before extending an invitation to speak with you. Stay calm and friendly and simply say, "Yes, it's true I don't have that specific experience. However, throughout my career I have had to learn new things and have always been successful." Do not ramble on trying to convince them. Be confident that you have a successful track record learning new things and they will need to decide if that works for them or not. Strength and confidence are key, and when a question likes this comes up, it will

provide you an opportunity to exhibit these crucial traits. Be sure to have one example of something you accomplished that you had not done before but successfully navigated.

5. The height of your bargaining power is <u>after</u> an offer has been extended.

At this point, you know you've eliminated your competition and the company is eager to have you join their team. Once you have reviewed the offer and have decided to say yes, this is the appropriate time to disclose any additional information that is now relevant to your new employer. For example, "I have had a chance to review the offer and would like to accept and select a start date, as long as you are okay with the fact that I will be on a family holiday from November 21st through November 28th."

Guardrail

Megan's analogy was a powerful way to re-think the way we approach interviewing. Included below are more specific questions and answers about common situations that may come up during the interview process. This guardrail will help you prepare and stay on track during an interview.

Q: How do I start?
A: Ask open-ended questions. Ask for the job description and find out if it is still relevant and accurate. "Is this still the most accurate reflection of the job that I'm interviewing for today?"

Q: What if they don't have a job description?
A: You can say something like, "No problem. If I was hired, what two or three things would I accomplish in my first year that would be a home run for you?" When they tell you those two or three things that they need to have accomplished, believe them. That is what you'll be spending your next year doing. They've just told you their pain point, and if that's not a fit for you, you've just found out in the first three minutes.

Q: How do I zero in on what I should be telling them about my experience? I only have a few minutes and there are so many important things to tell them about me.
A: As much as we'd like the entire interview hour to be all about us, it's not. Hopefully you've been listening to them talk up to this point and understand where their pain is. Only share the items on your resume that are relevant

to their pain. If they ask you a question about a specific bullet point on your resume, answer the question and then say, "Would you like me to give you another example of something similar I did at a different job, because it sounds like that skill set could be very valuable to your company?" Even though you've spent all this time preparing and summarizing all of your amazing accomplishments, and you've been immersed in making sure you can sell yourself, your goal for the interview is not to sit down and blurt out everything you've memorized about yourself.

Q: What if they ask me about something I don't have experience with?

A: Always be prepared to say some version of, "You're right, I don't have manufacturing experience." Then pause and remember, they called you. They already know that isn't on your resume and it wasn't a deal breaker or you wouldn't be there. Then say, "What I can tell you is that throughout my career I have had to learn new things and navigate change, and I've always been successful." That's it. It's very important to be grounded in that. In spite of all of your doubts and insecurities, they called you and wanted to meet you.

Q: How do I know for certain if I want the job, or not?

A: When you interview, your only priority is to get the offer. Then you can decide whether or not you want the job and either accept or reject their offer.

Q: What do I do when I get the offer?

A: You want to have an answer like this ready, "Thank you. I'm so excited by your offer and I look forward to reviewing it. I'll get back to you by the close of business tomorrow." Do not counteroffer or get into the details in that moment. You want to leave the conversation on a happy note and to be specific about when you will respond. If you propose marriage to somebody and they say, "Oh, I don't know. I'm not sure. I want to date three other people and then I'll get back to you," you would immediately regret asking them. Make sure that you have all the information you need. Did they tell you about the benefits? Do you understand how the bonus is calculated? Do you know how much it is going to cost you to insure your family? Make sure you have all the pieces to the puzzle. If the offer is great and you don't have any questions, call them and accept. But if you have any questions, the appropriate time to ask them is the next day. "I reviewed this, but I didn't see any details about how the bonus is calculated, and can you send me the benefits package with the monthly premium?"

If you do need to counter the offer, you can say, "The good news is, I've reviewed everything, and we're not that far apart." You may actually be a million miles apart, but you still want it to sound like good news. Then you can explain, "I was expecting $80,000 and you came in a little lower." Pause and listen to where they go next.

More important than anything, if you decline the offer because you got another offer and decided to take it, or maybe you tendered your resignation but your employer has suddenly found more money to give you, or the title you've been working for is now yours, whatever the reason, don't tell them exactly why you are turning down their offer. For example, "I sincerely enjoyed interviewing and meeting everybody and learning about your company, however, I've decided not to accept your offer."

It is a small world, and you never know when you might cross paths with this company or these people again. It's always best to simply say, "I appreciate the opportunity to interview. I have just decided it's not a perfect fit for me at this time."

Q: What about the offer? Does it always need to be in writing?

A: If the offer is verbal, you can say something like, "Everything you just shared with me sounds great. As soon as you can, please send over a formal offer letter and I'll read through it just to make sure there's nothing unexpected in it. I will get back to you within 24 hours."

Q: What do I say if they ask what my current salary is?

A: First, be familiar with the laws in your state. Some states have recently passed legislation that prevent employers from asking questions like these. If you truly have no idea what the position pays, and you're curious, you can say,

"If you can tell me what your salary range is, I can let you know if it makes sense for us to keep talking." This puts the onus on them to tell you. They may say, "We're targeting between X and Y," to which you can respond, "That sounds great. It certainly makes sense for us to keep talking." If they are waiting for you to respond, give them a broad range. If you were looking for $80,000-90,000, then the answer would be, "I've been looking at opportunities similar to this one, and the ranges seem to be between $80k and $100k, depending upon the bonus and the overall healthcare package." Targeting positions that are truly at your level helps because the other candidates who are interviewing will all be close to the same range.

Q: What if I want to accept the offer but I've got a vacation coming up and have already bought the plane tickets, or maybe I'd like to work from home on Wednesdays and Fridays?

A: The appropriate time to share anything about your personal life is once you have the offer and you're sure you are going to say yes. Do not bring up any personal information or requests like this in the middle of the interview process. Even if you're getting married in two weeks and you're in the final interview, don't say a word until you get the offer and accept it. It's not important. It's nobody's business until you've reviewed the offer and you're ready to say yes. Then you can say, "I've had a chance to review your offer, and I'm very excited to accept. I would love to pick a start date, as long as you're okay that I have a vacation booked from January 10 through 20th. **You have the highest bargaining power at the moment you're going to say yes, and that is when your personal life is suddenly relevant.**

The key here is that if they say, "I don't care. You cannot go on that vacation. We have three people out and we need you to be here on January 10th," you are still in the driver's seat. You can say yes or no. At that moment, you get to decide, do you want to cancel or postpone your trip? Or do you want to say no to the offer? Either way, you're the one in control if something like that happens. You might say, "You know, I'm super excited about this job, but I'd rather not cancel my vacation, so how about we cut a deal? I will postpone it to

June if you give me that week as an extra week off." Also, how that conversation unfolds will give you some insight into the culture of the organization.

I turned down my first job offer in San Diego. I was on the fence about whether or not I wanted to work at this company. I wasn't sure the culture was a good fit, but I was new to the city and I wanted to be working. It was mid-December when we were negotiating my start date. I let them know that I had already purchased a plane ticket to go back East and have Christmas with my family. They were adamant that I had to start on January 3rd. Throughout that conversation it became apparent to me that we were in a power struggle. Fortunately, I realized that quickly and had the confidence to say, "You know what, I think I'm going to pass on this offer. It's just not right for me." They were blown away that I said no, and I never regretted it.

Unwillingness to negotiate a start date could also be a red flag. It could mean they're understaffed, which is not good, or they have high turnover and they don't have coverage or the resources they need. It can give you important insight into the organization.

Q: What are some other tips before an interview?

A: Prepare. Research the company. Find out what they do, what they sell, where they operate. Check out their website. Buy something. There's so much information available on the internet. Look for recent press releases or news articles. If it is a company with a customer-facing retail store or a place of business where you can visit prior to the interview, go.

I've been in an interview where they've asked me, "Have you been to one of our stores? What did you think?" I hadn't been in one yet and planned to go after the interview. I could tell that the owner was offended.

The key to a successful interview is all about asking questions and listening, in order to find out how we can apply our experience and skills to resolve the needs of the organization. They have pain and we have the skills to treat it. Tricky questions don't need to trip us up and the number one goal of any interview is to get the offer. Then, and only then, do we bargain or negotiate personal terms.

Headlines

✓ Companies hire people who understand their pain and can help them resolve it, not people who try to tell them everything about themselves in an hour.

✓ The key to great interviewing is to always remember that it is not about you, no matter how much you wish it was.

✓ It is your job to focus on their pain and then share what knowledge and expertise you have that is relevant to that pain.

✓ If a question comes up that you do not have direct or recent experience with, how you answer is important.

✓ The height of your bargaining power is after an offer has been extended.

PART TWO

Execute Strategy

Management is doing things right; leadership is doing the right things.

—PETER DRUCKER

CHAPTER FIVE

DON'T BLOW A CIRCUIT

LEADERS ARE HIRED TO GET STUFF DONE

There is a lot of focus on leadership in our culture today and we often talk about the attributes of a good leader. In part one, we did the work of defining what leadership means to us.

What we don't spend enough time talking about is what leadership looks like on Monday morning, on Wednesday afternoon, in the conference room during a meeting, and when settling disputes about priorities or between co-workers. How do we model leadership in the trenches? How do we model leadership in the mundane day-to-day, when we're in the middle of a crisis and also when everything is going well?

HOW DO WE BRING OUR LEADERSHIP TO LIFE ON A DAILY BASIS AND AVOID THE FATE OF MY FRIEND'S FANCY LIVING ROOM?

Leadership is a common and coveted skill that Human Resources and hiring managers actively look for. Organizations know they need leaders. Why is this one skill so important? Why do we need all this leadership? **Organizations hire leaders for one reason—because they need us to get stuff done. They need us to execute on the strategy of the organization.**

The definition of the word execute is simply the act of completing a task or accomplishing a goal; to carry something out. The definition of the word strategy, in the simplest of terms without any corporate buzzwords, is a plan or method to accomplish a goal or set of goals.

IF WE'RE GOOD LEADERS, WHY AREN'T WE ALREADY SUCCESSFULLY EXECUTING STRATEGY?

Why doesn't this happen naturally? If we are such good leaders, don't we just automatically get all the important stuff done on a daily basis? If only it were that easy. What is it that gets in the way of our brilliant execution of strategy? In this section, we'll explore the top three reasons why we don't execute like we should, and then look at some solutions. You will notice that the solutions sound very simple, and they are. The challenge for leaders is being able to adhere to these principles on a daily basis. We will take a deep dive into each one and finish this section with some practical and hands-on guardrails that will help you on Monday morning, on Wednesday afternoon, in the conference room and in the hallway.

Often, leaders aren't executing strategy because we:

1. **Try to do too much.**
2. **Let the day-to-day priorities steal our time.**
3. **Do the wrong things.**

So what do we do instead?

1. **Resist the urge to do too much and limit your projects to no more than three at a time.**
2. **Protect your time.**
3. **Do the right things. Identify the projects and initiatives that will accomplish your goals. ONLY DO THOSE. Don't get distracted by good ideas. Be willing to pull the plug. Don't get off-track.**

These solutions are simple and sound like no-brainers, but stay with me. The complicated and challenging part is implementing and committing to these three things on a daily basis. Let's take a deeper dive into each one and understand what it takes to overcome these challenges.

LEADERS MUST RESIST THE URGE TO DO TOO MUCH OR THEY WILL BLOW A CIRCUIT

San Diego is known for its amazing weather but there is typically a heatwave that strikes every September. My husband and I relied on two freestanding air conditioners to keep our house cool. We discovered that if we ran the vacuum or my husband turned on the blow dryer in his art studio at the same time the air conditioners were on, we would blow a circuit. The lights went out. The cool air stopped flowing. Each one of those appliances functioned individually but when we tried to add another one that required a significant amount of amperage, it overwhelmed and overloaded the system. The amount of electrical supply or resources we had in our home was limited. Your organization works the same way.

What are the signs that your staff is close to blowing a circuit?

- Burnout. Listen to your people if they tell you they're overwhelmed. Take them at their word.
- Good people are leaving.
- Dissension and tension. Do employees dread coming to work?
- Core business is not getting done—customers are not serviced properly, phones are not answered, deadlines are missed.
- Strategy is not executed. Week after week your projects are stuck in the same place.

Organizations hire leaders for one reason—because they need us to get stuff done. They need us to execute strategy. Unfortunately, many organizations and leadership teams falter and struggle with this. One of the top reasons leaders aren't executing strategy is because they try to do too much.

WHY IS IT SO HARD FOR LEADERS TO RESIST THE URGE TO DO TOO MUCH?

There are so many good ideas.

Trying to accomplish too many goals at the same time is very common; I've seen it with every leadership team I have been part of. We sit in meetings discussing strategy with talented, intelligent people. We pull out the whiteboard or an easel with the adhesive pad so we can paper the conference room with our brilliant ideas. We try to narrow down to the top ten or five or three because we know we should, but then we create loopholes by loading up each initiative with sub-projects. We're only fooling ourselves.

Human nature

The second reason we try to do too much is, quite bluntly, ego. It is human nature, and part of our American business culture to want to be busy, to have so many projects that we spend our day in meeting after meeting and then the nights and weekends catching up on email and the day-to-day. It makes us feel productive and needed, which makes us feel important. It justifies our existence at an organization if we have a project to run. It gives us a reason to be invited to the important meetings and perhaps gives us an audience with the CEO or the Board of Directors. It is all ego.

We don't know what to do

The third reason is not one we talk about openly because it is embarrassing and comes from an uncomfortable place of vulnerability. The cold hard truth is that sometimes we have no idea what we should be doing to stop the bleeding of cash or the loss of customers, or grow top-line revenue or manage expenses, so we try different things to see what works.

But wait, why is it a bad thing to push ourselves to accomplish more than we think is possible? What about audacious goals, and stretching outside our comfort zone and moving our cheese?

Another reality that we don't like to admit to ourselves is that we overwhelm the resources of the organization when we try to do too much. Period. Most projects and initiatives take time, technology, cash and, most importantly, people to lead and to implement the project.

Here are some realities about these finite resources or amperage that we don't like to admit to ourselves:

Time. There is only so much time in a day or a week or a month. Regardless of the workaholic culture that we all pretend we love, time is still a finite resource. Your team has a limited number of hours that they can spend working. Even sixty hours per week is finite.

Technology. Your IT department, as wonderful as they are, can only do so much. They still have to support the ongoing operations of the business and troubleshoot daily issues with technology, which are unavoidable. It is the nature of business today. If the email server crashes, or the system freezes up, or the accounting team is locked out of accounts payable and inventory had a hiccup or the CEO forgot his password, it takes real time to manage and solve. More time than you think. Oh, and they still need to make sure that no transactions fell out on their way to the data warehouse, that credit cards only processed once without error, that shipping is able to print labels and that the postage meter is calculating correctly. They also need to get all the daily reports emailed or posted to the dashboard, even though only a few people look at them after the launch. Every single thing that happens in a business today needs IT to keep it running. In my experience, leaders significantly underestimate the amount of time this takes, and also underestimate the impact of projects on the IT department. Let's face it, they are on every project team.

Cash. Perhaps you are in one of those industries or organizations where cash is not a consideration. Personally, I've never worked for one of those. Cash management has had different meaning and priority in the various situations that I've found myself in. When I worked in the diamond jewelry business, we were highly leveraged and managed our line of credit on a daily basis. The amount of money I had available to pay vendors, buy inventory and spend on projects was directly related to how much I collected in receivables and whether or not it was a payroll week. Even in organizations that didn't manage cash this tightly, the budgeted cash flow was always a top consideration. As much as we all know that and recognize it, it is often the last thing considered when developing the list of projects for the year. I have a finance background so obviously it is always top of mind to me, but it should be for all leaders.

People. As with cash, perhaps you are in one of those industries or organizations where limited staff is not a consideration. Personally, I've never worked for one of those either. Most companies that I've been associated with or know of do not have the luxury of having a dedicated project team that has no other responsibilities other than the project they're assigned to. It is always the same people who are running and supporting the day-to-day operations who we also task with strategic projects. **We always underestimate how much time it takes for our teams to do their "day jobs" and how much free time they have.** Are there seasons and times when people have a little extra to give? Yes. It has always been my experience that most staff can be pushed a little to be more efficient with their day and can also fit in a project. But the issue arises when we try to do too many projects. You only have one IT department, one marketing department, one sales team.

Also, we underestimate how much time it takes to lead or manage a staff. We look at our top-level management and senior leadership teams and wonder what they do all day. Coaching, discipline, reviewing work, structuring priorities for the department, talking to third-party vendors and suppliers, and supervising the day-to-day all takes time. And don't forget negotiating who gets to take Christmas week off and determining whether Susy really disrespected Janet and whether Chad made a sexist comment to Lisa. It all takes much more time than you think.

You may still be asking, so what? Let's push ourselves, our teams, our resources to the brink, to the edge of what's possible. That's the only way to maximize what we can get. If you don't push people, you'll never get anything done. I'm not suggesting that we don't push people. I agree that, as leaders, we need to challenge and push. But we need to keep our expectations reasonable and limited, otherwise we will have the opposite effect from the one we want.

The amount of electrical supply and amperage we had in our home was limited. We had an older home and I believe our panel was 100-150 amps. This total available resource is divided up into different zones or circuit breakers. Your organization is the same way. You may have capacity in one department or circuit, but you may blow up your IT or Sales Department, depending on where you are burdening the load. You will get to a point where you blow the circuit and then nothing will get done.

HOW DO YOU FIND THAT BALANCE OF CHALLENGING YOUR TEAM TO ACCOMPLISH WHAT YOU NEED WITHOUT OVERWHELMING THEM?

Resist the urge to do too much. Many well-known strategy experts and philosophical time managers agree that three goals are enough. You have the reality of your day-to-day, a business to run, and you need to execute strategy. You have to leave time for all of this in order to be successful at both running your business and strategically moving the organization forward. The reality is, your organization and your teams will only be able to successfully implement a change or a small number of projects at one time. If you overload the team with too many things at once, they won't effectively focus on any single thing long enough to complete it or implement it the way it should be done.

Regardless of how passionate your team is or how convinced they are that they can do it, it is your job as their leader to limit the number of projects they take on.

Your Turn In The Seat

1. When have you experienced a blown circuit in your career?
    List examples.

2. How many strategic projects are happening right now in your
    organization? Do you recognize any of the signs that the team
    is overwhelmed?

3. What are the finite resources at your organization? What are
    their limits? Where do you see the risk of circuits blowing?

4. In your opinion, what is the right number of projects your or-
    ganization should limit itself to, based on your resources?

CHAPTER SIX

PROTECT YOUR TIME

The second problem we have that prevents us from executing strategy is that we let other things steal our time. Remember, time is a finite resource. I don't care who you are, how hard you hustle, or how much you brag about what little sleep you need, time is finite.

Most of the time, when our staff is assigned to a project or they hear the word "strategy," they roll their eyes, groan and commiserate with their co-workers.

"Here we go again…"

"Great. Just another time suck."

"I already have a day job, how am I supposed to find time to do this?"

Our staffs make comments like these because they've seen this before. Leadership returns from the offsite brainstorming session all pumped up with buzzwords, clichés and a list of projects and initiatives with owners and teams already assigned. It happens every year, sometimes twice a year. As I've mentioned before, I've been guilty of and complicit in this myself. The leadership team worked hard at that session to create a theme for the coming year, something so clever and brilliant that we are convinced our staff will be speechless and clamoring to help us achieve our goals. We love grand gestures and emotional, motivational department meetings where we attempt to inspire our teams around this vision of greatness that we had at the Strategic Planning retreat. We plan a kick-off event that feels like a political campaign rally with theme songs and balloons. We talk about audacious goals, 1 million customers, $1B in revenue, you name it, I've seen it. I've been on the committee that came up with corporate slogans like:

- Big Rocks (in the Mason jar).
- Rise Up.
- Building Our Future (we all got a toolbox and a hard hat).
- Hit the Damn KPIs.
- Venture Forward.
- It's Time 2 Believe (the 2B stood for $2B in revenue).
- Success Is Sweet! (the staff meeting was held at Hershey Park, PA).

Or, sometimes we hand out books and that becomes the mantra for the year. The CEO read a book that inspired them, so they order one for everybody and assign a reading schedule and expect book reports; books like *The One Thing*, or *Who Moved My Cheese*.

None of these are bad things. I get caught up in the moment too. I love to come up with clever acronyms and sayings. I get excited about change and the possibility to do things differently. A new fiscal year is to a business what a new calendar year is for us personally. We can be anything, do anything, this is our year. But the reason that staff members roll their eyes and sigh and whisper snarky comments to the person sitting next to them is because they know the excitement will wear off. We'll be gung-ho for a couple of months, our regular work will suffer, we'll have to put in more hours, and eventually the excitement will fizzle out. Eventually it feels like it was a waste of time, or we weren't really serious, or that we don't have the will to see it through.

But the reason the excitement wears off and fizzles out is not because the ideas were bad, or the strategic direction was off, or because the campaign was a dud. No, the excitement fizzles out because it takes a lot of hard work and focus to execute strategy. It takes consistent focus over time. We let other things get in the way and steal our time, and before you know it, six months have passed since the retreat in the desert, and we haven't completed phase I of any projects.

WHO OR WHAT IS STEALING OUR TIME?
1. **The day-to-day.**
2. **Fires.**
3. **Meetings.**

1. THE DAY-TO-DAY
Regardless of the type of business you are in, you have a very real set of day-to-day priorities that need to be handled. Customers call and need service and support; retailers have doors that need to open at 10 a.m. regardless of whether or not the manager showed up or the latest project has a deadline; manufacturing lines need their runs to be completed and shipped, even when the machine breaks down. Retail, wholesale, service, hospitality, event management and every other industry there is, has the very real daily work that needs to be done, and done well. Also, if you are a leader, you have a team that needs management. You need to handle performance issues, problem-solve, and set priorities. We already talked about how coaching, discipline, reviewing work, structuring priorities for the department, talking to third-party vendors and suppliers, and supervising the day-to-day takes a lot of time.

2. FIRES
In addition to our daily priorities, unexpected things come up. I can't tell you how many times I've started my day with a plan, a good plan, with time to strategize, analyze and check in with my team. Then the phone rang, or someone showed up at my door, or my boss called—before I knew it, it was the end of another day, I was exhausted with nothing left to give and I hadn't spent any time working on my strategic project. One Friday started out so lovely. I was able to get my workout in, had a cup of tea, and sat down to start my day. I only had two meetings on the calendar, which was very light, and I

had planned on completing my monthly board report as well as a financial model that the board had requested.

But then, during my 10 a.m. meeting, my phone and email began blowing up. I had three calls from the CEO plus email after email. A fraudulent transaction had been discovered, an important and well-known celebrity wanted to rent our facility on very short notice, a member of my team emailed her resignation letter, and I was discussing shutting down our business with more layoffs due to the pandemic. Before I knew it, the day was gone, it was 4 p.m. and I hadn't completed my board report or my analysis.

We've even coined the ultimate corporate cliché for this phenomenon— we call it "Fightin' Fires."

"Puttin' out fires" has become part of our culture. It is a badge of honor we wear proudly.

"How's your day goin'?" we ask each other.

"Oh, just putting out fires. You?"

"Same here."

I even had a boss once who loved to start fires. He loved to create chaos and watch us all scramble. He even referred to himself as an arsonist and actually thought it was an effective way to get his team motivated and working.

Fighting fires can also be fun. It's an adrenaline rush and when we're successful it feels good. We feel accomplished. I actually love it. I love to problem-solve and to do it in a high-pressure situation feels good. Sometimes it is the right thing to do but other times it isn't.

On that particular Friday, with my quick reaction and tenacity, we were able to stop the fraud and recover all of our funds, so that was a necessary reaction with a good outcome. However, multiple teams had a panicked reaction to the potential of the celebrity venue rental and stopped everything they were doing to prepare, only to receive word later in the day that the celebrity had decided on another venue in another city. All that firefighting turned out to be a waste of time and produced nothing for the company. We could have reacted differently to this particular fire. We could have discussed it and vetted it a little more. We could have let the celebrity know we were absolutely interested and would be ready if they chose us... but delayed engaging our teams and pulling them off course until we knew for sure it was going to happen.

The truth is, we like fighting fires because we're good at it, but more than that, we like it because it is more fun than sitting down at our desk and thinking about how to create change. If I have to go fight this fire, then I don't need to hold my staff accountable for missing another deadline or making another mistake. If I spend my day fighting fires, then I can wait another day to have that tough conversation to let someone know that their work has not been good enough.

 Firefighting is a welcome distraction that traps us in our sameness and keeps us from progress because when we're doing it, we don't have time to change.

3. MEETINGS

The third thing that steals our time and prevents us from executing strategy is meetings. We love meetings. You do. I do. They are necessary and they can be extremely effective in moving projects forward, resolving issues and managing our direct reports. A schedule or calendar of meetings also provides discipline and structure to our days. They give us purpose and keep us on track. I've used meetings for all of these reasons.

But there is also a dark side to beware of. Too much of a good thing can be toxic. For all the good they can accomplish, meetings can also steal your time and be ineffective. They can turn into glorified social gatherings and a waste of time for all involved.

At one company I worked at, we joked that we needed a bell that rang at the top of the hour, just like we had in school, to alert us when it was time to shuffle to the next meeting or the next conference room. If you needed to speak with someone, you hung out in the hallway and hoped to catch them between meetings. Almost on a daily basis I had to bring my lunch with me to a meeting because there was no time to eat at my desk. Some people tried to combat this by blocking their calendar so they wouldn't be invited to a meeting, but the trouble was, we all knew this tactic and invited them anyway. And the culture was such that you didn't turn down a meeting.

We all recognized it was a problem. We tried to fix it. We tried to streamline meetings and consolidate them. We appealed to the CEO to stop the madness. We talked about it, commiserated about it, and knew that it needed to change, but it was hard to actually pull the trigger on eliminating meetings. What are we so afraid of? I still don't know. I guess it is a version of FOMO (fear of missing out)? Or perhaps, like fires, meetings are a comfort zone or a distraction?

Most of the places I've worked have had a thing for meetings. My days were filled with meeting after meeting. I talk to my mother every day and give her glimpses of my work life, and she always asks me, "What are you meeting about all the time?"

You know the drill. There's team meetings and project meetings, status updates, one-on-ones with your direct reports and with your boss. We love meetings.

One of the silver linings of the current pandemic, I hope, is that corporate America will come out of this realizing that many things can be resolved without a meeting. Beware of virtual meetings, they are not much better. I have learned that screen fatigue is a very real thing and is similar to windshield time. It has always amazed me how you can drive for eight hours and be utterly exhausted when you finally wrench yourself out of the car. I never understood why windshield time is so exhausting when you are just sitting passively in a seat. You're not using any muscles other than your eyes and your brain. Turns out, that is exhausting. Screen time has the same effect. It takes just as much energy and time for virtual meetings.

If any of this sounds familiar, it could be a sign that your meetings have gone from useful to toxic and are stealing too much of your time.

Despite our amazing and smart leadership skills, we are not successfully executing strategy because we spend all of our time and energy, and all of the organization's resources, on REACTING to the day-to-day needs, demands, deadlines, customers, crises, and meeting invitations. If we are so busy reacting all the time, we are not being proactive or strategic.

HOW DO WE PROTECT OUR TIME?

We've established that the day-to-day demands are very real and must get done. That is a given. How do we overcome this "fire-fightin'" mentality? How do we find that balance with meetings so that they work with us to accomplish our goals and not against us?

1. Stop ignoring reality.

The reality is that most organizations run very lean, trying to get as much done with the least amount of overhead costs and people. They don't have the luxury of having a separate, stand-alone project team that can spend their days hanging out in cool and trendy project-management software.

The same people who are going to work on projects and execute strategy are the same people who need to wait on your customers, collect cash, sell your product, pay the bills—in other words, run the business.

When I worked in the retail industry, I witnessed this from the corporate view, but I've also noticed it as a customer, perhaps because I know what's happening behind the scenes. When you're in a retail store and the checkout or customer service line runs all the way to the back of the store, and you can see other employees ignoring the situation because they are busy doing other things, they are most likely working on projects—installing new displays or marketing signs, perhaps stocking inventory that someone in Corporate ordered so they could check a box on a new initiative. If you don't give the store the resources to get these things done, your customers suffer.

As leaders, you need to come to terms with and accept this fact before deciding on the list of projects/initiatives to be done. Stop ignoring reality. Be honest with yourself and your leadership team about the demands of the day-to-day and the strategic projects.

If you don't allow your team or yourself the time to do what you need to do, you are setting them and your organization up for failure, despite your amazing leadership attributes and good intentions.

2. React appropriately.

Yes, fires are real. We can't pretend they're not there. It's true that where there's smoke, there's fire. And if we don't react, the problem will spread and bad things can happen. Fires will erupt unexpectedly, be started carelessly, and may even be ignited intentionally. But none of that means you have to react. You're the Chief. You can spend some time investigating if it actually is a fire that needs attention. Is it really a problem? And if it is, is it a one-alarm, two-alarm, three-alarm fire? Obviously, they are not all the same. Even real firefighters have to assess the seriousness, the potential danger and risk, the severity and containment, and then determine the level of response that is appropriate. They determine if it is a one, two or three-alarm fire.

Employees, especially front-line employees, have a tendency to blow up problems and make them seem bigger than they are. It is usually all about perspective and point of view. If someone answers the phone all day, every day, and they field ten calls in an hour that all have the same issue—perhaps their shipment had the wrong item in the box—they could easily jump to the conclusion that there is a major problem with fulfillment of orders in the warehouse. The COO happens to walk by and asks them how everything is going just as they hang up the tenth call. They innocently let the COO know what's going on and use language like, "everyone," "system screwed up," "all the orders are wrong," and before you know it, a fire has been ignited. The COO goes immediately to the call center supervisor and tells them to notify the warehouse manager, the IT manager and inventory control. The fire seems to be spreading and within ten minutes there's an email or a phone call and an emergency meeting with twenty people to put the fire out. Did anybody take the time to ask how many customers were impacted versus how many orders went out that day? Did anyone bother to determine the scope? Or whether or not the danger was real?

If you have an employee who talks to customers all day and everyone they talk to is unhappy, they might start to believe that all customers are unhappy. And from their perspective, every customer they spoke with was unhappy. Are those forty unhappy customers important? Absolutely! You bet! And of course, you want your front-line employees reacting in the moment and taking care of that customer, and the next, and the next, as if their problem is the most important problem in the world. But there are 799,960 customers that they didn't talk to that day.

As a leader, it is your job to be able to discern that, yes, forty unhappy customers called today, but you have 800,000 customers...that's a pretty good average. Of course, all the customers who called were unhappy or canceling their order or membership. The obvious thing to remember, though, is that the ones who are happy and satisfied don't call.

Also, you can let a fire burn for a day or two. You can control and limit the resources that become involved—it doesn't have to consume multiple departments and disrupt priorities across the organization.

As a leader, it is your job to set priorities and to determine what fires need to be fought and when. Instead of a REACTIVE culture, you can design a smarter culture that takes a pause and spends five minutes thinking through whether or not you need to react right away. Play it forward. What will happen if you buy yourself some time before you react?

This tactic doesn't only have to be used with fires. It can also apply to daily priorities. Yes, it is the first Monday of the month and you need to email the monthly sales by sku report before 10 a.m. You've been doing it every Monday at 10 a.m. for seven years and three months. But what will happen if you are late this one time because you have an opportunity to get that person on the phone who you've been trying to reach for three weeks and is critical to complete the next step in your strategic project? If you miss sending out your monthly sales report by one day, what will happen? Will a decision be held up? Will another department suffer because you delayed this by 24 hours? Leaders need to reorder priorities and develop a culture around this key point. Oftentimes we freak out and panic if a report isn't completed or invoices don't go out on time. The truth is, your business probably won't suffer if a deadline moves this one time so that something strategic can be done.

It is okay if some things are pushed out, if it means that a strategic project or goal that will have lasting impact on your business can be moved forward.

We've all seen triage in action in our favorite "first responder" shows or movies. My first example was from the TV show, *MASH*. I was a child when it first aired but I still remember the high adrenaline scenes when the choppers landed and the doctors and nurses ran to the landing pad. Later on, I was a huge fan of the show *ER* which had the same type of dramatic scenes. During a major disaster or in an emergency room setting, triage is all about assessing multiple situations in front of you, getting as many facts as you can as quickly as you can and then setting priorities. This skill set isn't just for *MASH* doctors or *ER* personnel, it is also an important leadership skill. **Triage the fires and the daily priorities.** I once gave a presentation on this very topic at a leadership conference, and wittily pointed out that, "no one is dying" if you don't get the invoices out or finish that report. Sure, we all like to meet our deadlines, but the reality is, no one is going to die if we don't meet them because we took time to work on our project. A woman in the audience raised her hand and said, "Actually, I work in an intensive care unit, so somebody could die." I guess I need to find a new analogy.

3. Limit your meetings.

The third thing we can do to protect our time is to limit our meetings. How do we do this?

- Look for ways to consolidate meetings. Can you combine all the departmental updates into one two-hour meeting instead of ten separate one-hour meetings?

- Make the meetings you do have more efficient. Is your culture one where everyone feels the need to talk just for the sake of talking? Or do you only allow those with real news that would benefit the whole group to have the floor at a meeting? Is there a clear agenda for every meeting and a leader who is holding the group to that agenda? Have you invited too many people? Only invite those who need to be there—one representative from every department who can then go back and provide updates and feedback to their department. You don't need three people from IT or two from Finance or three merchandisers in every meeting.

- Create meeting-free days of the week, or blocks of time where meetings are prohibited. For example, no meetings on Wednesdays, or Monday afternoons.

- Create meeting limits for everyone in the organization. No one person can be in more than ten meetings in a week, or whatever the right number is. Limit the number of meetings that any one person can accept in a week. Once you've accepted ten meetings in a week you are locked out from accepting any more.

- Cancel recurring meetings that no longer have relevance. Check in with the attendees and discuss what you're legitimately accomplishing. Recurring meetings can outlast their original purpose and effectiveness.

Seriously. These are good ideas. Are they simple? Yes. Sometimes the answer is right in front of us. It is not easy to create this discipline and stick to it. But it is possible and if you sincerely do it, you will create a healthy culture in your organization.

If you want to successfully execute strategy, you must be realistic about your day-to-day demands, react appropriately to fires that erupt and limit your meetings. Structure your days and weeks and be intentional about your time. You're a leader, so I know you've studied time management. Back in the day, it was Franklin Covey's system that was all the buzz. I had a planner on my desk for many years. There was another system that was all about daily ranking of tasks and symbols you could use to organize your time. I'm sure there's an app for it today. Regardless of your system, you have to not only make the time to be strategic, you have to allow that same space and time throughout your organization and teams.

We protect the things that are important to us. We lock our homes at night because our loved ones are inside and during the day because we don't want to lose our 60" television. We lock our cars because they are expensive and we need them. We use passwords to protect our bank accounts and online activity. Our time is the most precious resource we have as individuals and as organizations. If you don't protect your time, it will be stolen from you. If you control your time, you control your day, and this will allow you to intentionally create the necessary space and time to do your day job along with your strategic initiatives. **As a leader, you must protect your time in order to carve out time for strategy, otherwise it will not happen.**

Your Turn In The Seat

1. Do strategic priorities compete with the day-to-day for you? List examples.

2. Is the culture in your organization and department REAC-TIVE? Are you a firefighter? Or a master of triage?

3. Do you ever turn down a meeting? Or block time on your schedule? What creative ideas can you take to your team to limit the time spent in meetings?

4. How can you create time in your daily schedule to accomplish your priorities AND your strategic projects?

CHAPTER SEVEN

DO THE RIGHT THINGS

The third item that prevents us from executing strategy is that we spend our precious resources, our time and money, doing the wrong things. Even good leaders can direct or allow a team to spend their hours and days on projects or initiatives that are not the right thing at that particular time. I know it's hard to believe, but I've seen this over and over again in organizations.

We do not start out our day, or week, or year, intent on wasting our time at work. But that is exactly what we are doing if we are not working on the right projects or priorities that will execute the strategy that we've determined is critical for our business.

HOW DOES THIS HAPPEN?
1. We get distracted by good ideas.
2. We don't want to pull the plug and admit when we're wrong.
3. We get off-track and can't find our way back.

1. Distracted by good ideas: How can it be wrong when it feels so right?

Has something like this ever happened to you? The last time it rained, you discovered a leak in your skylight when you got up in the middle of the night and stepped in a puddle of cold water in the middle of the bathroom floor.

A few weeks go by and the forecast is calling for an inch of rain so now it is critical that you take care of the leak. On Saturday, you have the day free, so you watch YouTube instruction videos while you drink your coffee and make a list of materials you need. You have a plan, and it's a good plan. You even got the ladder out.

Just as you're heading out the door to Home Depot, your buddy calls and tells you about the fire that started when the lint in his dryer vent ignited and gives you the play-by-play of how he put it out with his fire extinguisher, just in time before the whole basement went up in flames. After you hang up, you decide to check your dryer vent and discover that it has enough lint stuck to the inside walls to be concerning, so you unhook it, clean it out and while re-attaching it, you pop a hole in the vent pipe, so now you need to replace that. At Home Depot, you forget all about the skylight materials and only put the vent pipe in your cart. Right before you get to the register, your wife texts you, *Hey, while you're there can you see if they have one of those professional carpet cleaners to rent? The dog has smelled up the living room!* You were so close to getting out of there, but she's not wrong, so you head over to the rental counter and get the cleaner. As you pull into your driveway, you realize there was another text you didn't read, *Don't forget to get the carpet shampoo!* Damn. You head back to Home Depot and now two hours have passed since your buddy called. At this point, you are, as my father used to say, "burning daylight."

You need to get that dryer vent back in place because, unbeknownst to you, your wife had done a load of wash that morning and she needed to use the dryer but had no idea you were going to tear it apart. Also, she tweaked her back yesterday working out at the gym, so she asks you to clean the living room carpet. By the time you get the dryer back together and run the carpet cleaner twice to make sure you get all the dog hair, dirt and odor out, you are up against the four-hour rental limit and barely make it back to Home Depot in time. The skylight repairs are a distant memory and before you know it, the sun has set, it's time for dinner and some Netflix before bed. But you got a lot done today, so you feel accomplished and pretty good about yourself. You've made your family safer, and the house smells like lavender and babies.

Just after midnight, while you are comfy and cozy in your bed, dreaming of Sunday football and chili, the rain starts, just like the weather forecast said it would. The next morning you are jolted awake when your name is yelled as if the house is on fire and it's your fault. Your wife had sleepily trudged into the bathroom and slipped on the wet floor from the puddle that had formed when the skylight leaked overnight. Suddenly, you remember yesterday's well-intentioned plan to repair the skylight and become defensive when she says, "I thought you were going to fix this yesterday!"

"I was, but then Jim called and told me about the dryer vent. You don't want our house to burn down, do you?"

"What about after that?"

"You said you wanted the carpet cleaned, remember? I cleaned the carpet for you. Sheesh. Give a guy a break."

"But you knew it was going to rain and now we have a lake in the bathroom. And by the way, thanks to you, my back really hurts now."

Now, this may seem like a silly and lighthearted example, but this is exactly what happens in organizations. We can be easily distracted by good intentions and good ideas.

Perhaps you are losing customers faster than you can replace them, and your number one strategic goal is to grow your customer base. Everyone agrees. Growing the customer base will solve your revenue decline, which will in turn fix your cash flow and profitability challenges. You develop the list of projects and priorities that you believe will grow your customer base. You limit the number of projects to three so that you can execute well. You assign resources and get the projects started. But then someone on your leadership team gets an opportunity to partner with an affiliate for a new marketing program. They are an exciting, fresh and innovative company in the marketplace, and it's hard to say no. This project requires a daily interface with your website that requires custom programming, and in order to accommodate the reporting needs and bill the affiliate for the commission percentage, the accounting team needs to develop a manual process. The new program is confusing for the customers, so the call center volume of incoming calls has doubled and requires more staffing.

But it is such a good idea, and the CEO for the affiliate plays golf with your Senior VP of Marketing, and they convince both of their teams that this partnership must go forward.

As the year progresses, with this new, unplanned marketing program in place, you raise your hand at the monthly directors meeting and ask, "How's that program doing? Is it bringing in new customers?" Everyone turns to look at you as if you had just asked if anyone else had seen the spaceship over the bay last night. You hold your tongue, but ask the question again next month, and the month after that, and finally, one of the analysts has run the numbers. The affiliate marketing program is generating some revenue, but it doesn't appear to be incremental; the company is barely covering their costs; and most importantly, the customer base is not growing as a result of this partnership. Huh. You gingerly ask the next logical question, "Should we kill the program?" And you're met with that look again.

"Well, it's not costing us anything, really."

"Let's keep it going for another few months and see what happens."

"What's the harm?"

"The teams are so excited about it."

"You want to kill a program that's generating revenue?"

What is the harm with keeping this project going? The problem is, it is using IT resources, manual processing from the accounting team every month, eating up the marketing budget, and we already know that all of those things are finite resources. But the biggest problem of all is that this project is not doing anything to accomplish the strategic goal of the organization, which everyone agreed was to grow customers. Period.

The project you are working on could be "right" in so many ways, but wrong for you based on your strategic needs. Was it a good idea to clean out the dryer vent? Sure. Of course. But did it have to be done that day? Maybe Jim's dryer vent hadn't been cleaned in twenty years, or the fire started due to an electrical short. Just because it was critical for Jim doesn't mean it was critical for you. Was it a bad thing to shampoo the carpet? Of course not. Who doesn't love a fresh, clean carpet? But again, was that the best use of your time on that particular Saturday? No. Rain was coming and you had a leak. The number one thing you needed to do that day was to fill in the gaps around the skylight with silicone. The other two projects could have waited.

This sounds easy enough, at least on paper, but it is hard to say no to a good project or one that is requested by a senior leader in your organization, especially your direct boss or the CEO. Everyone may have bought into the concept and fiercely agreed to identify only three strategic goals at that planning conference in the desert. But it never fails, two weeks into the new fiscal year, more projects and ideas will be proposed, especially if you work for an entrepreneur. Entrepreneurs love ideas, and many entrepreneur CEOs feel that their job is to constantly generate ideas. Of course, this isn't a bad thing, in and of itself, but all ideas need to be vetted to determine if they are the right thing to do for your organization.

The CEO, senior leadership team and middle management may have come to a consensus that a particular project is the best thing to do, but if it doesn't specifically and intentionally drive you toward accomplishing a strategic goal of the organization, it is a waste of time, and if you continue to prioritize these types of projects or daily work, you will not be successful as a leader.

2. Don't be afraid to pull the plug

The euphemism, "pull the plug," can mean several different things. It can mean the tub is overflowing, so hurry up and pull the plug before we flood the bathroom and ruin the brand new porcelain tile floor. "Pull the plug" can also mean there's smoke billowing out of the vacuum cleaner, and the smell of burnt rubber is choking us, so pull the plug before we short a circuit or start a fire. It also means, in the most somber sense of the word, that it may be time to take Grandpa off life support and unplug the machine that is breathing for him, and ultimately end his life. Which we know is what Grandpa would have wanted.

When I was ten or so, I sat at the counter one day watching my mom make a cake. She was finished with the hand mixer, and began to remove the two beaters, but she forgot to unplug the thing first. As she was taking the first one out, the on switch slipped and the mixer kicked into gear. Suddenly her small hand was caught between the two beater blades and was twisting like cake batter. I froze, not sure what to do, when my brother's best friend, our neighbor Stephen, jolted into action. While I sat there with my eyes wide and mouth agape with shock, he jumped up and unplugged the damn mixer. Immediate relief washed over all of us, most of all my mom, as she untangled her hand and removed the beaters without any permanent damage.

Whether the project was a good idea in the beginning or just a distraction, you must be willing to pull the plug if it is not delivering the results you intended. It could be a pet project of your CEO, or a beloved tradition that no one wants to question. Pulling the plug can be one of the hardest things for leaders to do.

Our ego has a hard time admitting when we're wrong, but I think the ability to admit when you're wrong, or that a project you supported, piloted and brought to the table isn't serving the organization the way you thought it would, or isn't delivering the results you promised, is the strongest leadership move you can make.

Remember that scene in *Dirty Dancing* when Baby's father stands up and shakes Johnny's hand and says, "When I'm wrong, I say I'm wrong," and we all swooned? That move solidified our respect and love for Dr. Houseman.

Truly authentic leaders are not ruled by fear, are comfortable making mistakes and are strong enough to stand up and pull the plug. We need to be the ones who jump into action when everyone else is either twisted up in their own mess, or silently standing by knowing

there's a crisis but is either unable or unwilling to act. This is not weakness. It is strength. It is leadership.

Pull the plug.

3. Don't get off-track

On a Friday afternoon in September, my husband and I took our three little nieces to a pumpkin patch. They jumped out of the car squealing and took off for the hay bales, and the slide, and the sand pile. We struggled to match their pace and keep each one in our sights, to make sure they weren't in danger of hurting themselves, or worse, rudely cutting the line at the slide or being so loud others would give us the stink eye. There was also a corn maze. After they played for fifteen or twenty minutes, we thought it would be a good idea to walk the corn maze and then pick out our pumpkins and be on our way to what we had planned next. We thought the maze would be simple. After all, it was geared for children. There were no warning signs at the start, just a scarecrow holding a welcome sign and a jar to donate a dollar or two for admission. I think my husband and I were both complacent, so we didn't pay much attention as we entered the maze. Plus, I pride myself on having an outstanding sense of direction. I read maps for pleasure, and I am one of those people who likes to know where I'm headed, north or south, east or west, versus just listening to the commands from my phone app.

How hard could it be, anyway? As we started on a journey that we thought might take ten or fifteen minutes, tops, the girls were skipping and running ahead and Craig and I were leisurely following behind, not paying much attention to the path or the turns we were making. The girls were picking up corn stalks and using them as swords and walking sticks, laughing and teasing each other, while twilight was on the horizon. We hadn't a care in the world.

We came to a place in the path where we had to decide to turn left or stay to the right. We looked at each other and shrugged, convinced either one would lead us out. They wouldn't make this maze tricky, right? We turned left, but after a few minutes noticed we had gone in a circle. So next time we went straight, but again had to make a decision on left or right. Craig and I laughed and decided maybe we should seriously try to figure this out. We looked around, but the corn was taller than us, there was no one else around, and the girls were still having fun.

We began to pay attention and when we came to a fork in the path, we talked about it, weighed the options and then moved confidently forward. But we kept coming back around to the same place. After twenty minutes or so of doing this, and knowing that the sun was close to setting, Craig and I got serious. The girls could tell our tone had shifted and began to ask questions like, "Aunt Kelly, are we lost?" "Where are we going?" "I'm tired, can we go now?" I responded with things like, "Girls, stay close, hold my hand, stop hitting your sister, put down the corn stalks. No more corn stalks."

We started breaking off corn stalks intentionally and leaving them as markers so we'd know if we'd been there before. I began to listen for cars. With my amazing sense of direction, I knew that the main road should be on our right and that we couldn't get too lost if we found where the road was. Also, Craig suddenly remembered that there was a tall flagpole at the start of the maze, so if we headed for that flagpole, we'd find the exit. We began to work our way through the intersections, making choices that would lead us to the flagpole. Or so we thought. We saw the corn stalks we had bent over on the trail. The girls noticed too. Suddenly they were quiet and clinging to us. We eventually got close to the flagpole but realized that the pumpkin patch was nowhere in sight. Apparently, there were two flagpoles on this property. We turned back into the maze and looked for another way out. We left the trail at one point and took shortcuts straight through tall corn. Craig cut his toe on one of the sharp edges of the dried stalk. We told each other, "Worst case, we can cut through the stalks and head for the sound of traffic. We can walk back to the pumpkin patch along the road."

"It's fine. We'll be fine."

Eventually, I'm not even sure how we did it, we made a turn, and then another, to what looked like new ground, and as suddenly as we were lost, we were found again, and the exit appeared before our eyes. Phew! What was supposed to have been a fun, lighthearted, ten-minute jaunt, had turned into a slightly stressful half hour of "Oh my God, we need to get out of here with these girls before it gets dark." We had no idea the corn maze would be seriously challenging.

It can be the same way with strategic projects and initiatives in your company. You start out going in the right direction, but a turn here, a decision there, you're not really paying attention, and before you know it, you are off-track and not where you thought you'd be by now.

What can you do when you find yourself off-track with a project? You can stop moving until you know which way to go. You can look for markers. Stop moving long enough to run some numbers or analysis. Has what you've done so far produced the results you needed? Are you going in circles? Or do you need to adjust something?

As you commit to doing the right things in order to execute strategy, it is important to realize that what is right for you at this time might be different than other companies in your industry, in your executive focus group or what your golf buddy is doing at work.

RIGHT VERSUS WRONG IS UNIQUE TO EACH ORGANIZATION AND IS DETERMINED THROUGH ALIGNMENT WITH YOUR VISION, GOALS AND STRATEGY.

As leaders, we need to develop guidelines and guardrails to make sure that the ideas that turn into projects are the right ones. Guardrails keep us from going off a cliff, or from veering over the center line in the road into a head-on collision. The best way to keep people on the right road is to remind them, daily, if necessary, of what their goals are.

Next, I have two guardrails to share that I developed out of necessity when I was having trouble keeping people focused on the right things, the right projects.

Your Turn In The Seat

1. List your top three strategic priorities for the current fiscal year.

2. Now list your top three projects currently underway that are utilizing resources.

3. Do the projects align and support the strategic goals?

4. If not, what is the cause? Are you doing the wrong things because the project was somebody's great idea, and no one was willing to challenge it? Or did it start out well-intentioned and now no one is willing to jump up and pull the plug? Or did the leadership team get off-track and lost?

Guardrail

THE RED LIGHT GREEN LIGHT DECISION MATRIX

I come from the generation of kids that played outside all day, every day, during the summer as well as Saturdays and Sundays during the school year. I grew up in a rural neighborhood with a string of fifteen or so houses lined up on both sides of a quarter mile stretch on a state road. There were a band of kids that roamed from yard to yard looking for a game—basketball, tag, kill ball (this is where you just run around and bulldoze whoever has the ball), kick ball, or Red Light Green Light.

Red Light Green Light is not a complicated game. Its simplicity brings out the competitive drive to win, at least for me. There are no special skills needed. Anyone can do it. The main objective is to be the first to go from one end of a field to the other, without a ball or any kind of trick to perform. All you have to do is listen, stop when you're told to, and run like hell when you hear green light called out.

It's not a typical running race because you are stopped throughout the game and have to start over and over again. Therefore, the slow kids could win if they listened well and were able to stop on a dime. If you move after red light is called, you're out. It is all about listening to the caller's directions and obeying them. They have all the power.

The caller stood at the finish line at the far end of the field. The rest of us lined up at the opposite end on the starting line, with one leg forward, one back, knees bent, arms cocked, head up, ears perked, ready to go. The caller stood with their back to us and yelled out either "green light" or "red light." If they yelled "green light," we moved forward. Everyone had a different philosophy of how to play the game. There were those who sprinted with everything they had, and trusted themselves to be able to stop instantly, and were willing to risk being thrown out of the game if they didn't. There were those who moved steadily forward but controlled their speed, so they were able to stop with grass-blade precision when needed. Then there were the kids who were distracted, looking up at the clouds or shoving their brother off the starting line when the command was called, and were left behind saying, "What'd she say? I couldn't hear!"

If "red light" was yelled out, we froze instantly before the caller whipped their head around to see if they could catch one of us still moving. If we weren't at a dead standstill, locked in whatever position we landed in, we were called out and sent to the sidelines for the rest of the game. You were also out if the momentum was too much for your center of gravity and you fell to the ground while trying to stop.

The first one to the finish line won the game and assumed the role of caller in the next round.

As leaders in our organization, we help the team determine the red light or green light status of ideas and projects. We are the callers. It is our responsibility to ask the right questions to make sure that the ideas presented are well thought out and that they meet the self-imposed strategic goals of the organization. We have to play by our own rules.

We need to lead our team through a process in order to let them know if the idea/project/product is a green light or a red light. If you give the green light, the team needs to move forward swiftly and surely, and execute. If the red light is called, the team needs to stop on a dime. **As the caller/ leader, you need to be bold enough to halt the ideas that try to keep moving after the red light is called. The strength and survival of your organization depends on it.**

How does this guardrail work?

There is no shortage of projects or ideas on which to spend money. A recurring question resounds through many offices and conference rooms.

"Should we invest _____ in _____?"

Before you can answer this question, you have to set your rules of the game. What are your rules? We've all worked for companies whose main goal was to drive top-line sales or revenue. It is what we all dream about. This is an easy goal to get excited around and to gain consensus. It is easy to measure and track and can set the tone for the organization on a daily basis. If sales are up, the boss is happy, and so is everyone else. Happy boss, happy life. When sales are down, the mood changes. Depending on how long the downward trend lasts, the mood can range from depressed and paralyzed, to manic and desperate, and leaders can become surly, which never goes unnoticed by the staff.

But wanting to grow revenue isn't enough. It needs to be incremental revenue. If we are going to invest in a project, it must result in more sales than we would have had if we did nothing. Also, it needs to be profitable growth. If the idea on the table drives sales but is not profitable, you won't be in business very long. The same holds true for non-profit organizations with lofty mission statements. You have to bring in more money than you spend, or you won't be able to sustain serving your mission.

For purposes of this illustration, our rules are:

1. The project must drive revenue.
2. The revenue must be incremental.
3. The revenue must be profitable, organic and sustainable.
4. The investment required must be in the budget or we have to find the dollars elsewhere and offset.

When you are discussing and evaluating projects, ask whether or not the above requirements or rules are being met. If the answer is no to any one of these, it is a red light, and the project should be immediately sidelined. A yes answer is a green light, and the team can move forward to the next question. This process will help you determine if the project will execute your strategy.

Will the proposed project drive revenue? If the answer is no, it is a hard stop. If the project will not drive revenue, and that is the primary goal of your organization, then it is a no. STOP and move on to the next idea.

If the proposed project will drive revenue, there are still more questions to be answered before you reach the finish line. Those were the rules we set at the beginning. Keep drilling down until you've explored all the elements of a quality decision. The next question is, is it incremental? Will it result in more revenue than we would have realized if we didn't spend the money? If that answer is no, and it is quite often no, that is a hard stop.

If it is indeed incremental sales, is it profitable? Is it sustainable over time and organic to the business model? Compromising on these things is common because it is so tempting to do whatever you can to bring in more revenue. You can drive the top line all day long but if you're not making any money, you will not survive.

The final question is, is the spending included in our budget? If that answer is yes, great! **Green light**. If the project has made it this far in the analysis because it satisfies the rules and stays within the guardrails, we still have to find the dollars in our budget to fund it.

So many projects, but only so much time, and cash.

Therefore, you must have a discipline around quality decision-making.

I developed a worksheet, like the one on the next page, that I shared with the leadership team as a group and one-on-one every chance I had, or whenever a project was proposed.

Red Light Green Light Decision Matrix

Should we invest $1.2M in additional Inventory?

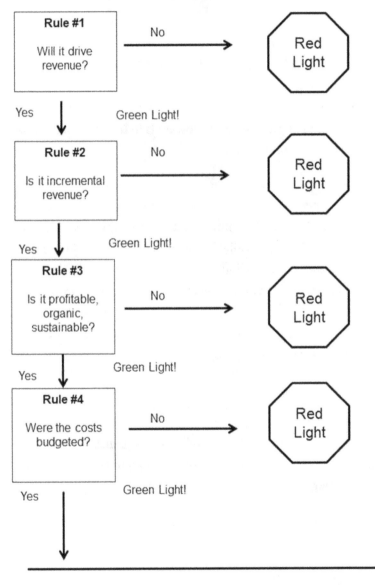

FINISH LINE!

Your Turn In The Seat

1. Think about one of your projects, priorities or goals. Use a past example if that is easier. Restate it in the form of a question at the top of the blank worksheet provided.

2. What are the important considerations that frame the goal? For example, revenue growth is important, but it also must be profitable. Is budget an important consideration? Or do you have extra funding available for projects? If cash flow rules the day, be sure to include that as a guiding rule. What are your clarifying questions for any project that is proposed? Perhaps you're not growing the top line but instead need to invest in infrastructure or meet a certain ROI. What are the rules of the game you've set?

3. Identify and define your rules for the Red Light Green Light decision matrix and fill in the boxes on the worksheet.

4. Evaluate your answers in number two against the rules in number three and fill out your own Red Light Green Light decision matrix.

5. Should you invest in this project? Why or why not?

Red Light Green Light Decision Matrix

Should we invest _____ in _____?

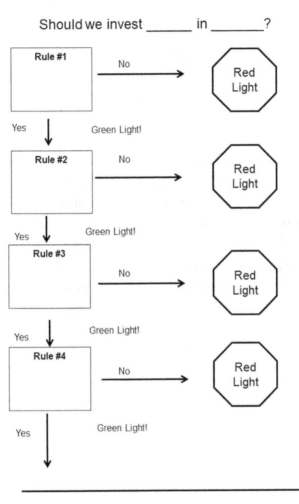

FINISH LINE!

Well done. You now have your very own decision matrix. This will serve you well. Hang it up in your office. Bring it to meetings with you. The next time you're sitting around a conference table or faced with a decision of whether or not you should take on a project, complete this matrix and find out whether it's a red light or green light.

Guardrail

THE CROSSROADS GRAPH

Another guardrail I've used in driving quality decision-making is this 2 x 2 graph. The strategic goal, in this example, is still revenue growth and is reflected on the Y, or vertical axis. Capital/Cost/Resources is reflected on the X, or horizontal axis and represents the most precious resource in the organization. It can be money, time or people. This tool will allow you to plot and map all of your current priorities/projects to determine where you may be headed off a cliff.

The Crossroads Graph

A simplified view of the crossroads between what you want to achieve versus what you are willing to give up to get it.

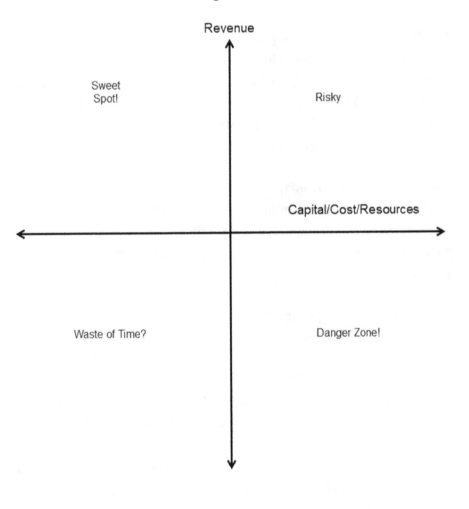

Risky (upper right)

If the project drives revenue, but it will cost the organization a lot in terms of dollars, people or resources, and it passed through the Red Light Green Light decision tree, it is still important for the team to understand the risks. Yes, it would drive incremental revenue, but it is going to require a lot from us, and we all need to be okay with that risk.

The Danger Zone (lower right)

If the project is going to cost a lot and it doesn't drive revenue, you are in the danger zone and need to get out as soon as possible. Avoid this area at all costs. At the end of this analysis, if you plot something in the danger zone and your CEO and leadership team still move forward, at least you've all been informed and have agreed to take the risk.

Waste of Time (lower left)

If the project will not drive revenue but it also won't require too much in the form of resources or people, is it a waste of time? Time is an often-forgotten-about precious resource. Our funds our limited, our bandwidth is limited, and so is our time.

The Sweet Spot (upper left)

Finally, those projects that drive incremental revenue AND don't require an unacceptable level of investment are the sweet spot. This is revenue productivity at its finest. You want these projects all day long.

This two-dimensional graph is a simplified view of the crossroads between what you want to achieve versus what you are willing to give up to get it.

As you move through a project, it may be necessary to revisit why you agreed to do something. When that question comes up, you can pull out your Red Light Green Light matrix or your 2 x 2 Crossroads graph and remind everyone how you arrived at your decision.

Both of these guardrails, the Red Light Green Light decision matrix and the Crossroads graph, will give you the courage, the platform and the support you need when the answer is no, and they will also give you the confidence and courage you need when your answer is yes.

Your Turn In The Seat

CASE STUDY

Fill out your own Crossroads graph, with your goal at the top of the vertical axis and your most precious and limited resource on the horizontal. Plot three or four projects on this graph and determine which zone you are in. Keep it with you for all those difficult decision-making conversations.

The Crossroads Graph

A simplified view of the crossroads between what you want to achieve versus what you are willing to give up to get it.

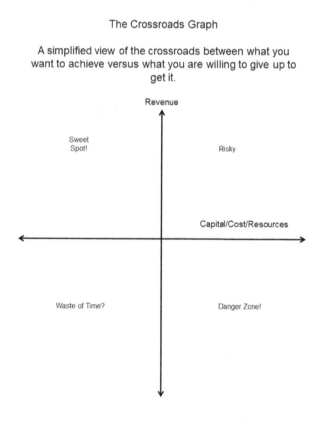

Headlines

✓ Leaders are hired to get stuff done. But it needs to be the right stuff.

✓ Resist the urge to do too much, protect your time and do the right things.

✓ Guardrails such as the Red Light Green Light decision matrix and the Crossroads graph will give you the courage, platform and support you need when the answer is no, and they will also give you the confidence and courage you need when your answer is yes.

✓ The reality is that you may or may not help develop strategy, and you may or may not agree with the strategy, but as a leader, you are here to execute strategy.

✓ All projects and priorities should help move the company forward toward a goal and to execute strategy. Otherwise, why are we doing it?

CHAPTER EIGHT

BONUS—CULTURE & PURPOSE

WHAT IS IT? WHY DO WE NEED IT? HOW DO I GET IT?

In the last twenty to thirty years in the business world, there have been plenty of buzzwords, books, theories and conversations about culture. It can be a polarizing topic, since there are those who love focusing on the culture of an organization and others who believe you can focus on culture to a fault, and it can destroy your strategy. The thing about culture is that if you don't intentionally create it, one will develop by default. Even if you are anti-culture and want to avoid any conversations about it in your organization, you still have one, whether you choose to recognize it or not. Regardless of where you are on the culture spectrum and how you feel about it, there is a living, breathing culture in every organization and wherever a group of people collects on a regular basis or around a common purpose.

An organization's culture is important and is more than just a cliché. Culture is our personality, both individually and corporately; it is who we are and what we believe about ourselves and the work we do; it is our character, who we are at every minute of the day; and the attitudes, goals and practices that make us unique. Our culture is the sum of many things, including our mission, vision and values. **Most importantly, culture is anchored in purpose.**

Culture is:

- Personality (individually and corporately).
- Who we are (what we believe about ourselves and the work we do).
- Character (who we are at every minute of the day).
- What makes us unique (attitudes, goals, practices).
- The sum of our mission, vision and values.
- **Anchored in PURPOSE.**

If you don't intentionally create a culture, one will develop by default.

CULTURE IS ANCHORED IN PURPOSE

St. Paul's cathedral in London was built around 1675 and designed by Sir Christopher Wren. The story goes that one day the architect, Sir Christopher, walked around the job site. No one recognized who he was. He began to ask the workmen questions. He asked the first stonecutter what he was doing. The stonecutter replied, "I am cutting a stone." He kept walking and asked another workman what he was doing, and the man replied, "I am earning money." Wren kept walking and asked a third workman the same question, "What are you doing here?" And the third man stood up straight, squared his shoulders, still holding his mallet and chisel, and replied, **"I am building a beautiful Cathedral."**

Was this last man also cutting stone and earning money? Yes, of course. But he assigned a different value to showing up every day. He connected his daily work to something greater. He saw what his co-workers could not. We all work. We all sign up to do different jobs intended to complete tasks. We need that. Our companies need that. We also do it because we get paid for it. We need the money. We need to pay for our homes and provide food for ourselves and our loved ones. Most of us are doing it for those reasons. But the third man in this story was able to connect what he showed up to do with something greater, something beyond just cutting stone and earning money.

Another popular legend has it that in 1962, President John F. Kennedy visited NASA for the first time. During his tour of the facility, he met a janitor who was carrying a broom down the hallway. The President casually asked the janitor what he did for NASA, and the janitor replied, **"I'm helping put a man on the moon."**

Take a moment to reflect on this idea. The janitor knew something that most of us struggle with. He knew the purpose of his work. He kept the building clean so that the scientists, engineers and astronauts could focus on their mission of putting a man on the moon. They did not have to worry about spending their time on trashcans, bathrooms or hallways. This janitor made sure of that. He saw where his contribution fit in the organization. He connected his purpose with theirs.

The stonecutter and the janitor both understood where their contribution fit in the greater vision, and it gave them **PURPOSE.**

Now I doubt that, in 1675, the work crew at St. Paul's Cathedral had a department meeting during which they brainstormed their culture and purpose statement, and I doubt that NASA had a three-step rollout plan for their purpose statement that engaged all employees. It just wasn't pervasive in our business culture at the time. The power of purpose hadn't been harnessed yet. But these two men were able to assign that value and purpose to their tasks for themselves. They had vision. Not all of us have the ability, perspective and language to do this. Plus, there's so much noise in our world and in people's lives that sometimes our teams need a boost, and they need help to connect their work to purpose. That's why companies hire leaders like us.

Purpose is connecting what you do every day to something greater than the task itself. Purpose is answering the question, why? Why do we exist? Why do we do what we do? And then connecting the task-oriented jobs we are hired to do with that Why.

How are you helping put a man on the moon? What is your beautiful cathedral?

WHAT'S THE BIG DEAL? WHY DO WE NEED PURPOSE?

Purpose matters and it is critical for every employee to understand their purpose, even more than the function they fulfill. It is important to be able to summarize purpose with a short sentence or phrase that provides a common language to all levels of staff. One that supports your mission, vision and values, and inspires your team to see beyond the tasks and functions they are responsible for.

I worked in one organization in the performing arts industry in which we managed and operated live event venues. We had a version of an Operational Excellence team that we dubbed the "Guest Experience" team. This team met on a weekly basis and focused on the guest experience, looking for opportunities to problem-solve, streamline and continually improve the experience for our guests and employees.

We concentrated on low-hanging fruit around the organization with projects that focused on communication, signage inside the venues, liquor license changes we wanted to explore and other customer-facing opportunities for improvement. It was exciting and fulfilling work, and most employees loved what we did and were happy to be a part of it. But we struggled with instilling a consistent and productive culture that reflected our mission, vision and values. Our culture didn't necessarily reflect how most of us felt internally about what we did.

Employees were dedicated but not always engaged. The team was competent and highly skilled in their areas of expertise but didn't always take ownership or display the team attitude and attributes that we knew we needed if we wanted to take our business to the level we desired. We knew that we needed an intentional focus on developing our Culture and Purpose.

In section three, we are going to learn that change is the intersection of discernment, discovery and determination, but this is a good example that will provide a little preview.

Our organization had discerned the change we needed. Then, the Guest Experience team set about discovering what that looked like for the organization. We knew that by connecting personal meaning to what we did, we would employ and engage people at a deeper level of commitment.

CLARITY OF PURPOSE AND CULTURE

During our <u>discovery</u> phase, we learned how important it was to learn our "why." We had an opportunity to leverage our passionate team of employees and take them to another level with a universal and common service motto or purpose of why we do what we do every day. We learned that best practice is to have a short sentence or phrase that provides common language to all levels of staff and supports the Mission, Vision and Values and inspires the employee group to see beyond the tasks they were hired to complete.

Your purpose statement should:

- ✓ Be simple and short and easy to remember.
- ✓ Reflect the mission, vision and values.
- ✓ Inspire all to see beyond the stones they are cutting or the floors they are sweeping.
- ✓ Answer the question: Why do we do what we do? Why do we exist? Why do people visit our business? What is our "man on the moon?"

Our team brainstormed this question and worked through the process to find the purpose or motto for our organization. We did this with a simple question: Why? Why do we exist?

Commit to working through this question as long as it takes to get the right answer. This is where the element of determination factors into the change you want to create. How do you know when you've found the right answer? *You'll know it when you find it.* Most likely, it won't be the first answer. You will need to push through the surface layer of clichés and first responses. In the performing arts organization, we dedicated time to intentionally and intensely talk through what we did and what it meant to us and our customers.

For example, we talked about how what we do means something different to everyone. Art is subjective. We could visit a gallery and all look at the same artwork, but we will all have a different perspective or response or reaction. I could fall in love with one painting that stops my breath, and stand in front of it, mesmerized, trying to fantasize about a way I could buy it and take it home. But someone else might look at the same painting and pass right by. It may even repulse them. Because art is subjective. We all approach it from a different perspective and viewpoint. We like what we like. We don't like what we don't like. That's just the nature of art. The subject of the art itself is not universally responded to. It's individual.

We talked about all of this as a team. We shared a story that we had heard from one of our vendors. She had told us about one of her favorite childhood memories of attending a performance of Yo-Yo Ma as a little girl with her mother and how it had moved her and changed her. We shared with each other our own personal stories of our favorite events—our first concert, mine was Loverboy; our first Broadway show, *A Chorus Line* when I was a junior in high school and our English class took a bus trip with scarce adult supervision so we got to run around Manhattan for the day; our first dramatic play, a mysterious show called *Back Bog Beast Bait* at Ithaca College. We began to examine the meaning behind what the arts mean to the community and the world at large and how it can be individual and collective. We talked about how you can walk into a football stadium with 70,000 people you've never met before and share an intimate experience listening to U2 or Blake Shelton or NSYNC.

IT IS IN THOSE MOMENTS, IN PLACES FILLED WITH STRANGERS, THAT WE FIND EACH OTHER.

Sharing experiences like this makes our world seem smaller and more connected, and at the same time these moments expand our vision and open up possibilities and new ways of thinking and being and moving through this world. We worked through all of this discovery to get to this purpose statement for our performing arts/live events organization: *We Create Moments That Matter*. It was simple. It was short. We could apply it to this performing arts business in a way that made sense to us and to our employees. The reality is that our customers, our patrons, and our employees, all experienced theater and events in a different way. But they all mattered to each individual. We felt that this purpose statement got to the *why* of what we did. We were there to create moments that matter for our employees, for our guests, for our patrons. We were sincerely satisfied and pleased with the outcome of that entire exercise.

Here are some examples of other purpose statements from companies you may be familiar with.

Ritz Carlton: "We are Ladies and Gentlemen serving Ladies and Gentlemen." According to their Gold Standards, this motto exemplifies the anticipatory service provided by all staff members. They have an accompanying credo, gold standards, mottos and a service strategy. Their entire goal is to exemplify the anticipatory service that they provide to their customers. All of their staff members are required to memorize this and buy into it, and they talk about it all the time.

Lego: Inspire and develop the builders of tomorrow.

Whole Foods Market: Our purpose is to nourish people and the planet.

Harley-Davidson: We fulfill dreams of personal freedom.

Ensuring the assembly line workers at Lego understand that the tasks they complete every day are "inspiring young engineers and builders" is an anchor. When the team is stocking shelves at Whole Foods or sweeping up a mess in the produce department or dealing with another customer complaint, they can come back to their anchor of purpose to "nourish people and the planet."

I can imagine the brainstorming at Harley-Davidson going something like this:

Leader: Why does Harley-Davidson exist?

Team: We sell motorcycles.

Leader: Why do we sell motorcycles?

Team: Because people want to buy them.

Leader: Why do people want to buy motorcycles?

Team: Because they're fun. Because they're cool.

Leader: Why are they fun? What do they represent?

Team: Rebelliousness. The fantasy/dream of an open road. Individuality. Being alone. Freedom. *Easy Rider.*

Leader: Bingo. We fulfill dreams of personal freedom.

HOW DO YOU BRING PURPOSE TO LIFE?

Now that you know what purpose is and why we need it, as with everything we learn in these pages of *Here to LEAD*, we need to know and understand how to bring it to life on a daily basis. As leaders, we know that is what we're here for.

You want your purpose to be the foundation or anchor of your culture. In order to do that, you need to find ways to engage people with that purpose every chance you get. Over time, it will become second nature and part of the fabric of your organization. It will be the foundation that your culture is built upon. What are some ideas or ways to engage your purpose?

1. Educate and communicate.

2. Service strategy.

3. Reward and recognize.

4. Acknowledgment and accountability.

1. Educate and communicate

The first step is to educate your team about what you are doing. Explain what culture is, and what purpose is. Let them know the process you went through to develop your purpose statement and share that statement with them. You may be starting from ground zero and at a place absent of culture, or you may be trying to change a dysfunctional one. Regardless, make a stand and be confident in your message. Communicate your next steps, and the ways you intend to bring it to life on a daily basis. Ask for help from your team. Ask for ideas. Remember, as leaders, we don't need to have all the answers, but we do need to provide vision and a common goal. It is critical to engage the leadership team first and solidify the purpose at that level.

Here are some ideas for this phase:

- ✓ Rollout/launch event.
- ✓ Tag line to be used in branding, website, social media.
- ✓ Email signature block: everyone in the company has a consistent email signature that reflects the purpose statement.
- ✓ Letterhead—tag line.
- ✓ Hiring, onboarding, training, orientation—there should be an intentional conversation about culture and purpose. Welcome letter to new employees.

2. Service strategy

A service strategy is another way to bring a purpose to life. We want to be able to bring that lofty idea that sounds poetic and lovely on paper to a real, raw, daily approach to our work. The importance of language when interacting with employees and guests (and everyone, really) must be considered. What does it look like when you are interacting with each other? With customers? With vendors? With the public?

The Ritz Carlton employs a "Three Steps of Service" strategy in which they commit to:

1. A warm and sincere greeting.
2. Use the guest's name. Anticipation and fulfillment of each guest's needs.
3. A fond farewell. Give a warm goodbye and use the guest's name.

Here are some other acronyms that outline a service strategy:

BRAVO (Body, Ready, Aware, Value, Own).

GIFT (Greeting, Interacting, Fond farewell, Thank you).

LEARN (Listen actively/repeat back, Empathy, Ask or apologize, Resolve the problem, Notify/report it).

3. Reward and recognize

- ✓ Make it daily practice to talk about, look for opportunities to communicate/reward.
- ✓ Include in team briefings.
- ✓ Signage in employee areas/break rooms.
- ✓ Buttons/stickers, employee ID badges.

4. Acknowledgment and accountability

- ✓ Build it in to conversations about performance, formally and informally. Discuss at weekly/month one-on-ones and also during annual performance reviews.
- ✓ Hold leadership accountable and address problems honestly and head on.
- ✓ Develop methods for staff to hold each other accountable.
- ✓ Feedback from customers—read your reviews; discuss with your team.
- ✓ Feedback from the team—provide a safe space for the team to discuss where they missed it.

Building a culture anchored in purpose results in engaged and empowered employees. Your employees need to know that their presence, in this moment in time, is invaluable to you, your mission, your culture and your purpose. You can't do what you do without them. The power of purpose can be experienced when engaged, empowered employees know not only what they do, but why they do it.

Guardrails

The following guardrails are examples of how you can bring purpose to life within an organization. A welcome letter provided to all new employees upon hire can set the tone at the beginning of your relationship and also remind hiring managers to have a conversation about culture during the onboarding process. A service strategy that all departments can customize to fit their unique contribution to the organization can be a powerful tool that provides common language and expectations. Finally, you can hold the team accountable with a performance review form, created from the service strategy, with space added for evaluation and feedback.

Dear Century Theatres Employee:

Welcome! We are so excited to have you working alongside us at **Century Theatres** as we fulfill our mission to deliver exceptional performing arts and educational experiences, and through collaboration and partnerships create an accessible place for all people to enjoy the arts at our historic and iconic state-of-the art venues.

We are in the performing arts business, and the thing about art is that it is subjective, extremely personal and means something different for everyone. Attending an event of performance art or theatre exposes us to worlds we've never imagined. The only thing we all have in common with **ART** is that it matters.

In your role here, you will help provide the physical space and the environment of excellence for guests to come and experience **moments that matter** for them and their families.

We believe that an organization's culture is important and more than just a cliché. Culture is our **personality**, both individually and corporately; it is **who** we are and **what we believe** about ourselves and the work we do; it is our **character**, who we are at every minute of the day; and the attitudes, goals and practices that make us **unique**. Our culture is the sum of many things, including our mission, vision and values. But most importantly, our culture is **anchored in purpose**.

At Century Theatres, we believe that purpose matters and that it is critical for all employees to understand our purpose, even more than the function we fulfill. We all want our work to matter. All of us need to know that showing up, day after day, means something to the organization, to ourselves, and to others.

Everything that we do—from keeping our venues bright and shiny and safe, to providing world-class customer service, to ensuring that our clients have everything they need to produce their event, to all the back-office tasks that are necessary but often invisible—everything is done in order to **create moments that matter** for our employees, guests and clients.

We expect our employees to bring this purpose to life on a daily basis through our **BRAVO** service strategy. We pay attention to our **B**ODY LANGUAGE or position, posture and politeness in order to convey respect and ensure access and ease of use for all who work at and visit our venues. We come to work **R**EADY or well-groomed, well-balanced and well-trained. We are **A**WARE of our surroundings at all times in order to anticipate the needs of our guests and fellow team members and offer an atmosphere of inclusion for all. Our knowledge delivered in a timely manner provides **V**ALUE, and we celebrate and exhibit our shared corporate values of collaboration and teamwork, diversity and inclusion, ethics and excellence with our team members, clients and guests. Finally, we **O**WN our contribution and purpose at Century Theatres by asking questions when we have them, speaking up when we see an issue, and solving problems with empathy and follow through.

Your presence here at this moment in time is invaluable to our mission, our culture and our purpose. We are so grateful that you chose to join with us as we **CREATE MOMENTS THAT MATTER** for all who enter our doors. Thank you for your commitment and passion. We couldn't do it without you.

Sincerely,

Jeanne Anderson
President & CEO

THE BRAVO SERVICE STRATEGY

The **purpose** of this service strategy is to clearly define the expectations for all employees of Century Theatres regardless of the role they serve. Century Theatre's purpose is to **Create Moments That Matter** for our employees, our clients and our guests. This strategy reinforces our pride of ownership and commitment to the Bravo experience and will guide team members to deliver a welcoming environment through exemplary service on a daily basis. The BRAVO acronym is used as an easy way to remember our service strategy and provide a tool to hold ourselves and one another accountable to these guidelines.

B Body Language

1. Position: We are physically present at our assigned location with an open, approachable and professional demeanor.
2. Posture: A strong posture promotes a sense of professionalism, readiness and expertise. We move with intention.
3. Polite: We engage using the 15/5 Rule. Within 15 ft., we make eye contact and within 5 ft., we smile and greet.
4. We respect bodies of all types and abilities and strive to ensure access and ease of working/attending for all.

R Ready

1. Well-groomed: We take care of ourselves with a neat and clean appearance so that our guests will have confidence that we'll take care of them.
2. Well-balanced: We are rested and healthy with the stamina we need to provide the attention and energy required for exemplary service.
3. Well-trained: We know what is expected of us at all times and seek and share information when we or our colleagues have questions.

A Aware

1. We are aware of our surroundings at all times; for example, we know who we're working with, and where the closest exit, radio or fire extinguisher is.
2. We anticipate the needs of our guest and team members.
3. We are consciously aware of how we can offer an atmosphere of inclusion for all people.

V Value

1. We provide value through fast access to knowledge and wisdom, convenience and respect of time, and ease of doing business.
2. We celebrate and exhibit our shared corporate values of collaboration and teamwork, diversity and inclusion, ethics and excellence with our team members, clients and guests.

O Own It

1. We "own" our contribution and purpose at Century Theatres by asking questions when we have them, speaking up when we see an issue, and solving problems with empathy and follow through.

Your Turn In The Seat

1. How would you describe the culture in your current organization? Culture is the sum of these things:

   a. Personality (individually and corporately).

   b. Who we are (what we believe about ourselves and the work we do).

   c. Character (who we are at every minute of the day).

   d. What makes us unique (attitudes, goals, practices).

   e. The sum of our mission, vision and values.

   f. Anchored in PURPOSE.

2. Does your current culture need to change? What about it would you like to see change?

3. What is your purpose statement? Does everyone at every level know this purpose? If there isn't one, spend some time brainstorming and drilling through your *Why*.

4. How do you (could you) bring this purpose to life on a daily basis? Here are a few ideas: Service strategy for customers; employee onboarding and training; performance review process; reward and recognition programs.

PART THREE

Advance Change

A leader takes people where they want to go.
A great leader takes people where they don't
necessarily want to go, but ought to be.

—ROSALYNN CARTER

CHAPTER NINE

WHY IS CHANGE SO HARD?

Ah, change…is there a more powerful, loaded, polarizing word in the English language? There are songs about change, quotes, memes, books, twelve-step methods, five-minute rules, four-hour bodies. We love to discuss, commiserate and encourage change and we love to find ways to trick ourselves into making it. On the flip side, we also fear it, hate it, and most of the time avoid it at all costs. It is both inspiring and frightening at the same time.

Alas, change is part of the human condition. We know we <u>can</u> change, we know we <u>should</u> change, we know change is <u>good</u> for us, but it is so hard, and uncomfortable, and unpleasant. These conflicting beliefs create cognitive dissonance within us, which sounds fancy, but we're all familiar with it. Cognitive dissonance is the state of having inconsistent thoughts, beliefs, or attitudes, especially relating to behavioral decisions and attitude change. It is going to the kitchen for a second chocolate chip cookie, because the gooey chips covered in sweet, soft dough are your favorite dessert, and you hardly ever have them anymore, while all the time you are saying to yourself, "No. Don't do it, Kelly. It's 300 calories. You have to weigh in tomorrow. You just gave up sugar for thirty days. Sugar is crack." But you do it anyway. That is cognitive dissonance. It's both wanting to eat the cookie and not wanting to because you know it's bad for you. Or it is lying on the couch all day watching SATC reruns or college basketball when you promised someone you would fold the laundry or sweep the garage. It's trying to avoid change at all costs, and at the same time knowing you can't or shouldn't.

WHAT IS CHANGE?

Change is one of those words, like leadership, that has many different definitions, depending on who is discussing it and the context around it. Like most challenging or difficult things in life, I like to spend time figuring out what it means to me. How do I define change? We spent some time talking about leadership and what it means to us, so let's do the same with change.

Change is opportunity and potential, new beginnings and better versions, exciting and dangerous. It is also hard work, often associated with loss, and will force me to give up something I like or love very much, or at the very least, have grown very comfortable with. You can see how cognitive dissonance is inherent in change.

The dictionary/official definition of change is: *To alter; to make different; to cause to pass from one state to another; as, to change the position, character, or appearance of a thing; to change the countenance.*

I've come to realize that:

CHANGE IS THE INTERSECTION OF DISCERNMENT, DISCOVERY AND DETERMINATION.

And because I'm an accountant, I always like a formula or math expression like, D to the power of three.

$$\text{CHANGE} = \text{DISCERNMENT} + \text{DISCOVERY} + \text{DETERMINATION}$$
$$\text{CHANGE} = D^3$$

Discernment

Discernment is the ability to recognize when a new way of doing something is necessary, either due to external forces beyond your control, or due to internal reasons. Change can be reactional or intentional.

Internal changes at work can be caused by many things. Perhaps the business is not performing as it should. We're losing customers or revenue for the 5th year in a row and cannot call it a fluke anymore; or spending is out of control and our cash is about to run out, or we've violated a bank covenant and our line has been called. Maybe one of our products is failing, or a disgruntled employee or customer has filed a lawsuit. Change comes with a new CEO or leadership team, a restructuring or acquisition. Perhaps it is just a new boss in your department.

Technology change, in the form of new system implementations and upgrades, is one of the most disruptive and disliked changes in organizations today. In my observation and experience, system changes can be some of the most terrifying that our teams face. Our patterns of behavior and how we show up every day and process invoices or journal entries, customer orders and complaints, or manage inventory become as comfortable as a pair of soft, out-of-style jeans that we insist on wearing on Saturdays because they feel good. I know exactly how they fit and have worn them so many times there are no surprises.

The list of potential changes is long and these things can happen in companies both new and old, large and small, public and private, and in every industry.

Change can also be external. The economic crisis of 2008 seems like so long ago now, but this was a great example of an outside force interrupting the direction and speed at which businesses were operating. I worked in the diamond industry then, and as a seller of luxury goods purchased with disposable income, we were one of the first industries hit hard and one of the last to recover. My ex-husband worked for a convenience store chain at the time, and they did just fine. In fact, they flourished. They were an essential business, and in tough times, people shop more at convenience stores. Wall Street professionals and hedge fund managers who were suddenly out of work had no bonus dollars to buy diamond jewelry for their partners. This crisis hit us hard and fast. I laid off two-thirds of our workforce in a single day, tried to keep the remaining skeleton crew focused and productive, and keep the doors open. We were in full-on crisis mode for more than a year. We were forced to change quickly. Our survival depended on it.

As I'm writing this particular chapter, the COVID-19 crisis has the U.S. economy hostage and has caused all of us to change immediately and radically. None of us saw this coming. We did nothing to cause it, we can't change what's happening and we can't control it or cure it, unless of course you are a scientist working on the vaccine. But it's changing everything. In the live events industry we were the first to shut down and will be the last to open. This particular change that has been thrust upon us is a great example of the loss associated with some change. We've lost many things because of this pandemic—people, jobs, income, a way of life—and we're all grieving in our own way because of it.

 The longer you deny or avoid change that you know is coming, is already here, or you know is necessary, the more dangerous and detrimental it is for you and your organization, and the harder it will be to ultimately advance change.

Discovery

Discovery is the second element of change. And for me the most fun. Once you've come to terms with the fact that change is imminent, you need to discover the solution, the new and improved way of doing something; you need to forge a path. As a leader, it is your job to find and uncover the solution, but that doesn't mean you must be the brilliant mind who creates it from scratch. As an authentic leader, I don't need to be the one with all the answers, I just need to be able to find the people who have them. The pressure isn't in having to think of everything, the challenge is making peace with the fact that you don't know everything and that it's okay for someone else to have the solution.

WE ARE MINERS, WORKING OUR WAY THROUGH THE NATURAL RESOURCES THAT SURROUND US, PANNING FOR GOLD UNTIL WE MAKE THE BIG DISCOVERY.

Determination

Determination is the superpower of change. You must have resolute willingness to persevere, push through and overcome all the challenges that you will encounter. Because change is hard. Discernment and discovery are the easy and fun part of change. **But determination is what puts change into action.**

Newton's first law of motion is that an object at rest stays at rest, and an object in motion stays in motion, continuing in the same direction and at the same speed until or unless another object with equal or greater force acts upon it. If we are the same as any other object in the universe, we are perfectly happy to keep doing what we're doing. We have a path, a routine. It's comfortable, it's known, it's predictable. **Whether we are at rest or moving, as human beings, we would prefer to keep doing it, uninterrupted.**

When change is introduced, it becomes the opposing object or force that will move us in a different direction, or at a different speed, and force us to change course or to start moving when we had been still. This takes more energy. Suddenly we have to learn a new way to move forward. We prefer the path of least resistance. If you've ever engaged with a teenager, either as a parent, stepparent, family member or friend, you are familiar with this phenomenon. Perhaps it is an unfair analogy, but in my experience, teenagers are the ultimate display of taking the path of least resistance, especially at home with their families. The funny thing is, they can usually step up to any challenge, but they're not going to unless it is demanded of them. Most teenagers I've known do not voluntarily take the garbage out. But they will if you ask them to umpteen times or threaten to take their phone away. Adults can be the same way in certain areas. We have teenaged blind spots too. It's really not our fault, or our teenagers' fault. It's physics.

We also tend to associate change with <u>loss</u>, even though we aren't always aware of it. If you are requiring me to change what I was doing, you must be asking me to give up or surrender something—perhaps it is my comfort or a tradition or even familiar dysfunction. Regardless of whether or not our current situation is working well for us, it is known. Change is unknown, and that makes us extremely uncomfortable. Have you ever tried to change a process or system at work that was extremely cumbersome and manual, but you were met with resistance? Your team was actually mad at you? And you couldn't believe it because you just made life easier for them, or so you'd thought. This new way is so much easier, but instead of slapping you on the back and saying, "Thanks, man," they glare at you and whisper behind your back, "Who does he think he is?"

The third reason that change is hard and requires determination is because, if you are asking me to change, or I'm asking myself to change, we often jump to the conclusion that it must be because I was wrong about something. In order to accept change, I have to admit that what I was doing is no longer working, or perhaps it never was a good idea, and I just couldn't see it.

Change requires humility and vulnerability, and both of these can be hard for us human beings to stir up. It means owning the fact that we don't know everything, sometimes we're wrong, and sometimes there is a better way. That is hard to admit regardless of who you are. When someone approaches us with change, we go into defense mode. We put up barricades and walls with our stubborn grip, refusing to let go because to let go would be to admit that we failed.

More than twenty years ago, some of my family was hanging out at a friend's place on the river. It was sticky, hot and buggy, so we all took relief in the cool water. Our friends had a Tarzan rope hanging from a tree on the riverbank and we took turns getting a running start, jumping on to the rope and swinging out over the river doing our best jungle call, Aah-eeh-ah-eeh-aaaaaah-eeh-ah-eeh-aaaaah!

Of course, once we reached the middle of the river, we'd let go of the rope, plunge into the water and swim out of the way of the next swinger. It was my dad's turn, and as we all stood by and watched, he got a running start, latched on to the rope and swung out over the river. He didn't let go when he was supposed to and swung back over the concrete pad where he had launched. He still had enough momentum to swing back out over the water, though. We laughed and yelled, "You gotta let go, silly!" Then we watched as he held on for the second time and came at us again, his eyes wide, mouth closed. He was still moving but it was clear that the rope was slowing down and he was slipping lower and lower on it. "Let go. Let go, Dad! Let. Go. Of. The. Rope." But he didn't. He came back in the last time swinging so slow and low on the rope that he scraped his shin and foot across the concrete and began to bleed. He gashed his leg open wide and ugly. Someone grabbed the rope this final time and stopped the spectacle. To this day, none of us knows why he didn't let go. He doesn't either. He hung on for no good reason and it ended up hurting him.

All three of these things—physics, loss, our ego—make change one of the hardest things for us and our teams. That is why we need that superpower of determination.

Change is always personal for these reasons. Regardless of where the change is coming from, or what is driving it, we take change personally.

I heard a pastor say once in a sermon, "When change is necessary but fails to occur, a crisis will emerge." Historically, we've seen this happen in our culture in areas such as civil rights, racial injustice and homelessness. In a broad sense, we've been resistant to change in these areas and crises have emerged in the form of riots, civil unrest and an overwhelming problem to solve, in which the richest country in the world has men, women and children floundering on the streets without shelter and a reliable source of food and care. All of these social crises developed because change was necessary but failed to occur.

It is human nature to dislike change and to avoid it at all costs.

REGARDLESS OF HUMAN NATURE, CHANGE IS A NECESSARY REALITY AND WITHOUT IT, CRISIS WILL OCCUR.

Not only do our teams need bold leaders to help them through the internal and external forces of change, it is one of the reasons you were hired or placed in a leadership position. As leaders, we are expected to advance change in our organization and within our teams.

Leading an organization through change, positive or negative, will be one of the most challenging things you do as a leader, but can also be one of the most rewarding. Leaders advance change.

HOW CAN WE MAKE CHANGE HAPPEN? CAN WE JUST HAVE A MEETING AND ANNOUNCE IT?

It would be nice if we could just have a meeting, send an email or set a date on the calendar, announce the change we need and everyone would say, "Yes, I'm in," and change would materialize exactly when and where we need it. Unfortunately, that's not how it works. Change happens when we are committed to these three things:

1. **Operational excellence.**
2. **Bold decisions.**
3. **Time.**

CHAPTER TEN

OPERATIONAL EXCELLENCE

WHAT IS IT? WHY DO I NEED IT? HOW DO I GET IT?

We've established that change is often a reaction to internal or external forces. It can also be purposeful and intentional and part of the culture of the organization, department or team.

The term Operational Excellence by itself sounds abstract and lofty. Here's how I define it:

Operational Excellence is a way to create intentional change before it becomes a crisis or barrier to executing strategy, growth or business continuity (sticking around for the long haul).

It is a philosophy or culture where problem-solving, teamwork and leadership focus on improving the daily activities in the workplace, in order to serve the customer and meet the needs of the business, while keeping the employees positive and empowered in the process.

Still sounds abstract and lofty, right? The question remains, why do we need it and how do you do it? How does it become part of the fabric of an organization? What does Operational Excellence look like on a daily basis? **Before we get in to how, let's talk about why it's important.**

In previous chapters, we've discussed how precious our resources are. Our cash, our technology or IT resources, our time and our people. These things are on limited supply. If we are not spending our time doing things in the most efficient and excellent way, we are wasting precious resources.

When I was growing up, my family had a vegetable garden. It was approximately the size of a large rectangular swimming pool, maybe fifteen by thirty feet or twenty by forty. It seemed giant to me and it was big enough to hold rows of tomatoes, potatoes, corn, peppers, lettuce, beans, peas, carrots, spaghetti squash, yellow squash, dill that my mom used in canning all those vegetables, and even corn stalks around the edges and random sunflowers. My mom was the supervisor of the garden, and her five kids were the maintenance crew. We worked it. Anyone who has ever grown and maintained a garden knows how much work they are. It takes planning and consideration of what you're going to grow and how much space you will allocate for each thing. How many rows and which rows will be what? All of this planning takes place beforehand. Then you buy your seed packets or plants and set about the hard work of planting. Once that is done, you can stand back, hands on your hips, smug smile on your face, satisfied with yourself and the work of your hands. Then wait. Wait for it all to sprout and grow and produce crop. It's time for you to enjoy the fruits of your labor.

If only it were that easy. Unfortunately, now it's time for the real work to begin. In other words, making sure that all those seeds and plants have enough resources to live a healthy life so they can produce. They need sun and water and healthy dirt. If rain doesn't come, you have to water diligently or your plants will dry up and eventually die. You have to protect your crops from outside predators like deer, rabbits, rats and insects. You may have to put up a small fence or use some other organic and healthy methods to keep those things from eating or destroying your crops. Finally, you need to keep the weeds at bay. Weeding your garden is not fun or glamorous. It is hard work that takes commitment, sweat and, as my dad used to say, a little elbow grease. He'd also say, a little hard work never killed anyone.

We do not plant weeds, they just show up. A weed is a plant in a non-desired place, an aggressive reproducer; unwanted. Weeds may be unwanted for a number of reasons: They might be unsightly, or crowd out or restrict light to the plants we do want or they might use the limited nutrients from the soil. They can harbor and spread plant pathogens that infect and degrade the quality of crop or horticultural plants. Some weeds are a nuisance because they have thorns or prickles, some have chemicals that cause skin irritation or are hazardous if eaten, or have parts that come off and attach to fur or clothes. **Regardless of whatever their specific harm might be, weeds are bad and we need to keep them away from our garden or they will choke the life out of everything that is good and green.**

OPERATIONAL EXCELLENCE IS TO AN ORGANIZATION WHAT WEEDING IS TO YOUR BACKYARD GARDEN.

It is hard work, is not always fun, takes discipline, commitment and the right tools, but it is necessary in order to get the results you want. If you ignore a garden for a length of time, it will become overrun with weeds.

You can't start a company, spend all the time planning, obtaining funding, hiring people, putting processes in place, and building your business, then just stand back and do nothing to maintain it. You have to try to prevent weeds, hoe the garden, and if necessary, get down on your hands and knees and pull them up at the root.

A culture of Operational Excellence will give you the discipline to uncover and uproot weeds that have the potential to choke the life out of your organization.

This is especially critical in organizations that have been around for any length of time. Sometimes the lot is so overgrown that your only choice is to bulldoze and spread fresh seed. Other times it is not so far gone and you can actually go in and hoe the rows and perform maintenance to keep the weeds out. It may be that you need to get down on your hands and knees and do some back-breaking work with your gloves on, pulling the weeds around the bean plants or the pepper plants or the lettuce. Operational Excellence can help you with all of this.

What are weeds in the corporate sense?

Examples of weeds in the business world are processes that require high effort but have little impact or ones that are cumbersome, manual or perhaps just no longer necessary or fruitful, but nobody wants to cut the cord or pull up the root.

Operational Excellence will keep you nimble and ready to react, ready for the deer, rabbits and insects, the external forces that come your way, such as an industry disruption or a pandemic. During the pandemic, businesses that already had remote working as part of their culture were able to quickly adapt.

Operational Excellence will keep your organization healthy and productive. If you can't manage the day-to-day processes in an efficient and effective manner, how are you going to execute strategy, advance change and drive results? Also, weeds make your team miserable. And if you want a healthy, productive group of people running your business, you need to keep the culture, atmosphere and daily work life healthy. No weeds.

Operational Excellence will position you for growth. If your processes are cumbersome and manual and labor-intensive, they are most likely not scalable. So how are you going to grow? How are you going to handle the 20% increase in customers if your onboarding process is a mess? How are you going to meet the shipping demand of an increase in revenue if your warehouse inventory is so inaccurate that you're selling things you don't have in stock?

NOW THAT WE'VE ESTABLISHED WHAT OPERATIONAL EXCELLENCE IS AND WHY WE NEED IT, THE REAL QUESTION IS...

How do we do it? What does it look like on a daily basis?

1. Get buy-in. Accept that you need it. The first step is to make a conscious decision to focus on Operational Excellence with the senior leadership team acknowledging how important it is to your organization, your department, your team. Get buy-in.

2. Get a room. Get the right people in the room. Set up a recurring meeting schedule. This is the planning process. We are mapping out our garden.

   In the last three organizations I've worked in, I've created a cross-functional, cross-departmental team that met regularly for the sole purpose of focusing on Operational Excellence. Typically, you want a representative from accounting/finance, operations, sales, customer service and IT. Build whatever team makes sense in your company or industry. The point is to have input and ownership throughout and across the organization. As I mentioned in the introduction, I was named VP of Operational Excellence at the company I worked for in Boston, just before I moved. The CEO had recognized the importance and impact of Operational Excellence and was committed to assigning resources to it. In the next two companies I worked at, the leadership was on board as well. Once you have an understanding with senior leadership and they're confident you have a plan and a purpose, they'll be on board. Who doesn't want a nimble, healthy and productive organization that is positioned for growth? We all do, of course.

   Remember in **Part Two, Execute Strategy**, we talked about things that eat up our precious time, and one of those was inefficiency and too many meetings. Make sure that this recurring meeting of stakeholders focused on Operational Excellence is productive. Have an agenda and stick to it. Start and end on time. Keep the conversation moving. Limit your list of open items, park the rest, and as you complete projects, bring a new one in from the parking lot.

3. Weed. Now we must set about finding the weeds and uprooting them. Just like in a garden, this is where the hard work is.

Once you have the team assembled, even if that team is just you, there are specific ways you can find opportunities for Operational Excellence in your organization and there are some things to look out for. This team needs a leader. You need to lead them through this process.

Five ways you can find opportunities for Operational Excellence and develop a list of projects are:

1. **Pay attention.**
2. **Be creative.**
3. **Change the conversation.**
4. **Partner with people.**
5. **Challenge the process.**

1. Pay attention

Nobody likes a complainer, especially leaders. We are, by nature, allergic to negativity and avoid it at all costs. We're trained to ignore those who see things as half empty. Most leaders I know are optimistic by nature and avoid people they consider whiners, complainers and negative forces that can suck the life out of you.

However, I challenge you to listen when your staff complains and is frustrated. Instead of immediately writing it off as negativity, vet their complaints and determine if there are valid points among the whining. Chances are you will always have negative, pessimistic people around, but sometimes your team is complaining for a valid reason, but they don't have the perspective or language to express it as clearly as you might find useful. They may not be fluent in the corporate buzzwordy clichés that we've all learned to accept and communicate in.

Someone might walk into your office, drop a report on your desk and say, "You need to find someone else to do this. I don't have time to do Joe's job and my own. Not my problem anymore," and then walk out. You're left speechless, not quite sure how to handle this obvious disregard for your position and glaring disrespect. What looks like a childish temper tantrum could be a symptom of a process in dire need of an Operational Excellence overhaul. Your team member didn't have the language or skills to say, "I'd like to circle the wagons on the monthly usage report with the appropriate stakeholders, because the output doesn't seem to match the level of resources required and there seems to be a glitch in the process. Could we set up a meeting to discuss?" More importantly, this team member has been complaining about this report and process for months and has been ignored.

I was working as VP of Finance and I kept hearing how awful this one particular process was in marketing. It had to do with tracking member rewards or points. This wasn't my area of responsibility or my department, but I kept hearing this junior staff member talking about it. One day, I started asking her questions about the process. She explained how she was downloading data into this monster spreadsheet that she had to populate and maintain, and described all the errors that ensued. I didn't have an immediate or magical solution for her, but I had heard enough and knew there had to be a better way. I connected her with one of the analysts on my team who was a data/Excel whiz and asked him to help find a solution. And they did.

Learn to listen actively and respond intelligently. On another occasion, one of my colleagues with whom I was having lunch was explaining this onerous process of documenting the team's retail customer visits. They typed notes in Word documents and stored them on the shared network, but the sales team had a hard time finding the notes when they were on the phone with the customer. I was in finance, she was in sales training, I had heard in one of my Finance/IT meetings that our ERP system had the functionality to upload documents and attach them to a customer account. When she took a bite of her sandwich, I chimed in with, "You know you can upload documents in our ERP system and attach them directly to the customer account, right? They'd be right there for the sales reps." This blew her mind and changed everything.

Listen. Pay Attention.

2. Be creative

Be creative in finding solutions. Creative thinking and brainstorming can sometimes be hard for your analytical, operational team members who are drowning in day-to-day details and fires. They need you to lead them in brainstorming sessions.

The best way I've found to brainstorm is to keep drilling down further and further into a problem that needs solving, or an idea that needs vetting, by asking questions. As the leader, your role is to keep the team asking questions and challenging the status quo. Once you do this, stand back and let the conversation unfold among the subject matter experts. Oftentimes they will arrive at some great solutions and will become excited by the process. When they get stuck, you step in with prompts and questions to keep them moving. Don't accept any answer at face value or assume it's right. Take nothing for granted. Sometimes the question to keep asking is as simple as why? Or why not?

When I was seven or eight years old, my mom hired a babysitter, Veronica, Ronny for short, who smacked me hard across the face one day because I asked her *why* too many times. Then she put me in solitary confinement for the rest of the day. I sat in the middle of an empty room with the door closed for hours. I don't remember the specifics, but apparently, she had had enough of me asking why, and I suppose it was a habit I had developed or was trying out. I guess I'm still that annoying, inquisitive girl who always wants to know why—especially when it has to do with why an organization is able or unable to do something.

Be sure to foster a culture of curiosity and permission to ask *why* within your team. Let it become a habit to ask why or why not? Don't be like Ronny.

3. Change the conversation

I know you've experienced this: You're in a new position or perhaps a new company, you see an opportunity and ask the question, "Hey, why don't we _____?" And you've received the standard answer, "Oh, we can't do that because _____."

I've heard all of these and more:

- "Our system can't do it."
- "We cannot program any changes because we're on an old version that's not supported anymore."
- "Yeah, good idea, but we can't because the shipping software doesn't talk to order-entry."
- "We don't need to. We have a work-around."
- "We've never done that!"
- "That would take way too long."
- "We don't have the bandwidth or resources."
- "If we do that, we'll lose customers."
- "Good luck with that. Merchandising won't like it."
- "I don't remember why, I just know we can't."

All of these are tactics to avoid the hard work of change. Most of these excuses are also rooted in fear. We were proposing a new email marketing campaign for an exciting new event. The marketing director was resistant and very vocal about it because of her fear that customers would unsubscribe to our mailing list. It took some conversation and work to convince her that we could run a test and monitor subscription rates, and then pivot if we needed to.

Interrupt. Change the conversation. Responses such as the ones above become habitual. Don't let the team get stuck at all the reasons why they can't do something. Instead ask, what <u>can</u> we do? If we don't have the bandwidth or resources, is there something else we can take off the list? What are we doing that is a waste of time? How can we find resources within the company?

It can be difficult to get people to approach a problem differently. You may have to ask these questions over and over again and at several junctures. But eventually, the team will catch on and shift their thinking.

This dynamic reminds me of the parable of the elephant. I don't know if it's a folktale or a true story, but the story is that fully grown elephants can be tethered in place with a small stake and thin cord. This defies all logic. The size, power and ability of the elephant allow them to easily uproot the stake and break the cord. But because the elephant was tethered as a calf with the same small stake and cord, and tried to break free but was unable to, they never try again. The elephant believes this stake and cord are enough to hold them the rest of their life. When I hear teams reciting all the roadblocks and reasons why we're unable to do something, I think of this story. **As leaders, it is our job to yank the stake out of the ground and break the cord in order to show our teams what they are truly capable of.**

4. Partner with people

Find and listen to those who have good ideas but are not implementers. Every organization has them. There are plenty of team members who know how things could be done better or differently, but they don't know how to garner resources to get them done. If you are having a hard time improving a process or finding a solution to a problem, go talk to the people on the front line.

If there is a problem with shipping or returns, walk the warehouse and speak to the workers who spend their days picking and filling customer orders. They may have great ideas and the solution for how to be more efficient, but they are not in a position to get any momentum going. Invite them to come to your team meeting and share their ideas. Then, you lead the team to get it done. You'll be amazed at the creative ideas and answers that are lying dormant in every department throughout the organization. The people with the right answer may lack confidence, or not have the authority or position to move an idea forward, or perhaps they do not possess the necessary project management or leadership skills. **That's why you're there. Lead them.**

5. Challenge the process

Look for those things that take high effort but have little impact. Many times, especially in established organizations with a lot of longevity in the team, processes can continue in perpetuity, and we just keep them going and going and going, and people rarely ask, "Hey, does anybody still use this report that I'm spending half my day on?" "Is this information still relevant or useful?"

Many organizations have daily, weekly, monthly or quarterly reporting that teams are responsible for producing. Our email inboxes are flooded with them. One time, I asked the producer of one such report, "Who is this for?" and he responded with the name of someone who hadn't worked at the company in almost ten years. When I pried further and asked who was reading it today, he couldn't tell me.

We can get into a pattern of producing, and at times, entire positions and departments are built around it. **We're afraid to ask if someone still needs the report we're producing, because that means they might not need us.** But it is necessary to ask, to challenge. I would bet money that countless hours are burned on a daily basis churning out reports that either nobody needs, nobody reads or nobody uses to make a decision. Ask each department leader to document why they are doing each process that they do. Who is it for? Who needs it? What is the benefit? If they can't answer those questions, they are on autopilot. Stop doing it for a week or two and see what bubbles up. That might give you some clues. Be brave enough to challenge.

1. **Pay attention.**
2. **Be creative.**
3. **Change the conversation.**
4. **Partner with people.**
5. **Challenge the process.**

All of these are ways to find opportunities for improvement, to unearth the weeds. Remember the guardrails—keep your meetings efficient, on track; keep your list small. It is a marathon, not a sprint. And just keep working. Keep hoeing. Keep weeding. You're never really done.

All of these strategies mentioned above, when focused on repeatedly, will become habit in your organization. Over time, your team will learn that it is safe to engage in all of these behaviors. You can create this culture within a team and by extension, the whole organization.

"We are what we repeatedly do. Excellence, therefore, is not an act, but a habit."

—WILL DURANT

Creating and committing to a culture of Operational Excellence will free up resources, improve the customer and employee experience, and streamline and scale processes, which will ultimately position your organization for the future and for growth, and will allow you to accommodate change in whatever form it comes.

Guardrail

OPERATIONAL EXCELLENCE SUMMARY

I. What is it?

Operational Excellence is a way to create intentional change before it becomes a crisis or barrier to executing strategy, growth or business continuity. It is a philosophy or culture where problem-solving, teamwork and leadership focus on improving the daily activities in the workplace, in order to serve the customer and meet the needs of the business, while keeping the employees positive and empowered in the process.

II. Who is it?

A cross-departmental team that identifies opportunity and focuses efforts to drive operational excellence throughout the organization and is critical to creating and maintaining a culture of operational excellence.

III. How is it achieved?

(What does this look like in an organization? What does it look like in your organization?)

- Pay attention. Listen when people complain and are frustrated.
- Be creative in finding solutions, ask why not?
- Change the conversation. What <u>can</u> we do?
- Partner with people. Find those people who have good ideas but are not implementers and partner with them to do it—if it makes sense.
- Challenge the process, especially those with high effort but little impact.

IV. Why is it important?

Creating and committing to a culture of Operational Excellence will free up resources, improve the customer and employee experience, streamline and scale processes, which will ultimately position the organization for the future and for growth.

V. In summary:

1. Gain buy-in from senior leadership *(hint: use this one-page summary)*.
2. Get a room with the right people in it.
3. Start weeding.

Your Turn In The Seat

1. List three to five complaints that you've heard repeatedly from your team, or anyone in the organization. Bring one of your complainers in and ask questions. Be curious. Be open. What did you learn?

2. Can you think of any processes in your organization with high effort but low impact? Do you receive any reports that you toss in the recycle bin without even reviewing, or emails that are deleted before they are even opened?

3. Are there any areas where you are stuck? For example, are there issues you keep talking about over and over again that have no apparent solution?

4. Are you actively working on Operational Excellence in your company? What steps can you take, in your current role, to introduce this discipline? Can you start in your department or team, or perhaps recommend to senior leadership a cross-functional, cross-departmental team? Is it already happening and you're not part of it? How can you get in on the action?

CHAPTER ELEVEN

COURAGEOUS DECISIONS

Courage is not the absence of fear or uncertainty, but is instead taking action in spite of it. Change is necessary, unavoidable and one of the hardest things to face as individuals and as collective teams within a corporation. Of course, it causes fear and uncertainty, and we're not immune to these feelings just because we are leaders. Courage is being afraid and doing it anyway. **As leaders, we will need courage to make the decisions necessary to advance change.**

Change does not occur in a flash or in a moment in time. It does not happen in a meeting or in a conference room with the best and the brightest, or the highest earners, seated around the table.

There is no instant change. It is a process that happens at the decision points.

CHANGE COMES FROM MAKING DIFFERENT DECISIONS THAN YOU'VE MADE IN THE PAST IN SIMILAR SITUATIONS.

Courageous decisions are both the big-ass, strategic, monumental decisions that set strategy, direction and vision, and the smallest decisions that are necessary to keep you on course. In some ways, it is easier to make the big, life-changing decisions. The real work, the real, lasting change occurs in the day-to-day, moment-by-moment decisions we make. At every decision point, we have an opportunity to create the change we've already said we want and know we need, or to retreat back to the status quo.

It is the decisions we make that determine whether we will remain comfortably at rest on our current path, or whether we will allow the force of change to do its work.

It is a big strategic decision to say that you are going to travel to Alaska in 2022. Great. You made that big decision. But guess what? You haven't moved anywhere yet. You need to choose how you are going to get there. Car? Train? Airplane? When are you going to go? And for how long? Where will you stay? Where in Alaska will you go? Making the grand decision to visit Alaska in 2022 is just the beginning of making it happen.

I am one of those people who has lost the same twenty pounds many times in my middle-aged life. I know how to do it. I know what I need to eat or not eat and how much. I know that working out alone won't do it for me. I know that I hate to count calories. I know how to lose twenty pounds. I've done it many times.

I've also learned that writing in my journal, "I'm going to lose twenty pounds by Memorial Day" isn't enough. It's great to begin there. It is important to have a vision, and to write it down and meditate on it. To decide to do it. It is even better to have a plan on how you're going to get there. But guess what? Thinking, journaling and planning, while necessary, is not what change is made of. Doing these things every day will not lose twenty pounds for me.

The real change, the real loss, will occur in the choices I make day by day, moment by moment. When my alarm sounds at 6 a.m., will I get up and work out? Or will I roll over and put if off another day? When someone brings chocolate chip cookies to the breakroom, will I cave? If I eat one, will I decide that the diet is out the window and proceed to consume chocolate chip cookies until I am sick? Or will I decide to consistently eat the healthy food that I wrote about in my plan?

Our choices either protect or compromise the decisions we have already made.

REAL, LASTING CHANGE OCCURS WHEN THE DAILY CHOICES YOU MAKE CONSISTENTLY PROTECT YOUR DE-CISIONS OVER TIME.

Change comes with every choice we make and action we take. If you make the right decision to begin with, and then act on it enough times with protective choices that align with that decision, you will change yourself and your organization.

How do we make courageous decisions and leverage those to advance change?

Using courageous decisions to advance change is a three-step process.

1. **Make the right decisions (quality decision-making).**
2. **Make choices that protect rather than compromise your decisions.**
3. **Know when to fold 'em (be courageous enough to pivot).**

1. Make the right decisions.

Quality decision-making is one of the most critical skills necessary to acquire as a leader and a discipline that you need to develop in your team. Not only are these skills necessary in the context of allocating resources, they are also critical in advancing change. Utilizing a decision matrix, like the Red Light Green Light or the Crossroads graph in chapter 7, will ensure decisions align with and support strategic goals. In order to advance change, we also need to understand how these two factors impact our decision-making process.

- Analysis paralysis: Avoid the idea that analysis must be perfect to make a decision. 80% is good enough.
- Business acumen.

Analysis paralysis: Is it corporate legend? Or is it a real phenomenon?
It is real. Analysis paralysis is the inability to move forward with decisions until or unless the analysis is perfect, perfectly error-free, risk-free, all-

encompassing (meaning every possible scenario in the world has been run and every variable considered), so that all parties can be confident that the decision is not a mistake and nothing bad will come from it.

Have you ever been asked to prepare an analysis in preparation for a strategic meeting where important decisions were going to be made? You worked your butt off getting the numbers right and looking good on your spreadsheet and graphs. You did the very best you could possibly do with the information at your disposal. Perhaps you engaged your team to help or they did the bulk of the work and you reviewed it. You made color copies and brought the stack of stapled reports to the conference room and nervously waited for your turn on the agenda to present your masterpiece. Everyone was waiting for the analysis and perhaps you felt pressure to have it line up with and support the idea on the table or the proposed project.

You cut the stack in half and handed out the reports to the people on the right and left of you to pass around the table. As you waited for everyone to receive their copy, you rehearsed the key points in your head and were bursting to finally share what you'd been working on for weeks and weeks. But before you got through the first page, someone noticed an incorrect number, or asked a question that you hadn't considered or prepared a scenario for. Your chest tightened, your palms began to sweat, your stomach knotted, you began to stammer and try to convince everyone that those points are minor and wouldn't change the outcome, but they all stopped listening. The senior leader in the room went off on a tangent, or took out his HP12C or iPhone, and started adding up every number in your spreadsheet to check your subtotals.

You never got the crowd back, and they tabled the idea or decision until you could run some more numbers. You scheduled a date two weeks out to reconvene and review another deck of spreadsheets. The decision was delayed because imperfections were found in the analysis. But what if we considered the idea that, in general, if the analysis is 80% correct, it is good enough to make business decisions?

Often, an obsessive focus on perfect analysis, also known as Analysis Paralysis, is a way to avoid the hard work of quality decision-making and advancing change. As leaders, we need to understand this, look out for it and avoid it. Instead of avoiding the decision, we need to avoid analysis paralysis. As the name suggests, it will cripple your team, your organization, and prevent change.

This is especially tough for those of us who have an accounting and financial background. However, if you want to add value and be a strategic partner to your company and senior leadership team, you need to balance the accuracy and discipline necessary in most aspects of accounting and finance with the analysis used to support strategy and advance change.

Payroll, taxes and financial statements need to be 100% right. Account reconciliations, audit records and payments made to vendors need to be accurate. But the four different scenarios you put together to determine whether or not additional inventory will drive sales or whether or not you should add benefits to your membership plan does not need to be 100% perfect to make a decision. Eighty percent is good enough. If you spend all your time getting the analysis perfect you will have missed your window to make the right decision at the right time, or perhaps you will avoid making a decision at all.

This phenomenon is very common and can be tricky to communicate to a junior team. You want to instill accuracy in their work and don't want your position to be miscommunicated and used as an excuse for lazy or sloppy financial analysis.

Avoiding analysis paralysis and understanding that 80% is good enough to make decisions is a discipline that needs to exist at the leadership level.

Perfection in business is not an achievable or reasonable goal. It is a deflection and avoidance tactic that leaders often use in order to avoid the risk of making decisions. Don't be that leader.

Business acumen

Business acumen is sound insight and judgment used to quickly understand business risks and opportunities, which allows you to confidently provide input and to develop strategy and make decisions. This is a skill that will be developed throughout your career with the mentoring and leadership of others, by your own mistakes and successes, and from partnerships you form with colleagues and industry professionals.

- Watch and listen, observe and witness: see how others do it.
- Talk it out with yourself, your friends, others you respect.
- Learn from your success and failure. Take notes.
- Join and participate with colleagues and industry groups. They can be a wealth of information and invaluable, non-risky sounding boards.

2. Make choices that protect rather than compromise your decision.
Courageous decisions must be supported and sustained in the daily, ordinary choices that we are faced with:

    a. Despite resistance from teams.
    b. Despite pushback from customers or other third parties.

Because change is hard, you will receive resistance and pushback from your team, your colleagues, your leadership, and your customers and vendors. Whoever is impacted by the change will resist it at first. It is human nature. But if you truly made a quality decision using your tools and the information/data at your disposal, then you must not waiver. This is where the courage comes in.

It is the choices you make after the decision is made that will determine if the change you desire will be realized and how long it will take you to get there.

This is why quality decision making is so important. The quality decisions you make are the foundation you need on which to balance your confidence and courage. Remember in the section on executing strategy we learned that using solid tools to make decisions that align with our strategy are critical and necessary to allocate resources. But this is also critical to advancing change. Your courage needs to be balanced on solid, quality decision-making. The choices you make in the moments will either compromise or protect the quality decision you just made.

When you encounter resistance, it may be necessary to revisit why you agreed to do something. When that question comes up, you can pull out your Red Light Green Light decision matrix or your 2 x 2 Crossroads graph and remind everyone how you arrived at your decision.

Remember, your decision-making guardrails, like the Red Light Green Light decision matrix and the Crossroads graph, will give you the courage, the platform and the support you need when the answer is no, and will also give you the confidence and courage you need when your answer is yes. They will also give you the courage and confidence you need when you encounter resistance and are tempted to make a choice that compromises that decision.

I began a new CFO role many years ago in a small manufacturing company. I heard team members talking repeatedly about how they couldn't rely on our system to check inventory levels. It unsettled me. Why would you have an inventory system that you couldn't rely on? I mean, what was the point? So I started asking questions and drilling into the issue. Nobody really knew, or could articulate, what the issue was, other than it was just wrong. When a customer called to place an order and wanted to know how long it would take, the employee had to put the phone down and go to the warehouse to check on the physical items on hand before they could commit to an order. It was extremely inefficient but had become accepted over time as "just the way it is."

I knew I couldn't accept this or be responsible for it. I saw quickly that one of the issues was that they only performed a physical inventory once per year. When I asked why it wasn't being done more frequently, I was told, "It takes too long," "It's impossible," "We'll never reconcile, so what's the point?"

Fortunately, I had hired an operations manager who shared my problem-solving nature and was willing to challenge the status quo with me.

We announced that we were going to perform a physical inventory at every month end. We were met with resistance, anger and mocking. But we forged ahead and stayed committed to our decision. The first few months were painful. The counting process was cumbersome and it did take too long. The variances were significant, more than 10% of the total inventory value on the balance sheet, which was hundreds of thousands of dollars. I was horrified, but was met with the response, "We've tried to find the reasons and the cause but haven't been able to. It's just the way it's always been."

We were relentless and, over time, as the team began to see that we meant business and were going to keep doing this, they began to take it more seriously. Throughout the month, as we were processing purchases, orders and shipments, they began to view every transaction through the lens of, "How will this impact inventory?" and "Will this create a variance at month end?"

We looked for ways to streamline and speed up the counting process. Since this change wasn't going away, everyone adapted. The team became anchored in this new perspective and began to pay attention and be less careless throughout the month in their maintenance of inventory records and transactions. They realized it was much easier to research and troubleshoot the variances within a month versus trying to go back and reconcile a whole year. When I left that position, our monthly variances were negligible and a fraction of what they had once been. Because of our new process, if a significant variance did occur, we were able to zero in on the issue to swiftly and confidently resolve it. By making this courageous decision and not relenting, by not compromising, we built a discipline and process that the organization had not experienced before.

I once worked for an organization that was struggling with brand awareness and had made it one of their strategic initiatives. One of the objectives was to improve how marketing dollars were spent. They were a manufacturer with a network of retail customers that carried their product in their stores. It was customary in this industry to provide co-op advertising and marketing dollars to the retail customers. Our leadership team made a very sound decision that we needed to have better structure and guidelines around how those dollars were used in order to ensure that they were effective in building our brand. It was our money, after all, and the decision was unanimous.

We all left the conference room feeling great about ourselves and the decision we had made. We developed the guidelines and sent them out to our customers. But then...the first customer called, resisting our new guidelines. Of course, they wanted to spend the money how they wanted to spend it, using the funds to build their own business. We stuck to our guns. But then they threatened to return all of our merchandise. **That was the beginning of the end of that particular decision.** The salesperson went to the VP of Marketing, who then went to the CEO. The organization was so afraid of losing that one customer that they backed down. They told themselves it was just that one time. However, as soon as you waiver on your decision one time, it becomes easier to waiver the next time. Your team sees this and they conclude that you didn't really mean what you said. When the next customer called, and the next, we kept making exceptions and very soon that quality decision we'd made in the conference room, and the new guidelines we'd developed, were dead in the water. Guess what happened? Nothing. We did not move the needle on increasing brand awareness or meeting our marketing goals. The change we had committed to, and knew we needed, did not happen.

Effective leaders need to make quality decisions that align with strategy, and when confronted with the in-the-trenches resistance to those decisions on a daily basis, they must choose to protect rather than compromise the decision. Courage isn't the absence of fear. Courage is acting even though you are afraid. You don't need courage in the conference room. You need it when facing the customer. You need it on the phone calls. You need it facing employees and colleagues.

Imagine what would happen if TSA officers caved on their rules and guidelines every time an airline passenger got upset or threatened to never fly again if they couldn't bring their coffee on board, or their weapon, or their oversized suitcase? The airlines developed their rules for sound reasons with a goal to improve the safety and security for all passengers. They can't afford to bend, and neither can leaders.

Often, this type of scenario can play out in changes in leadership or new hires. About six months after I was brought in as CFO at the small manufacturing company that needed a lot of infrastructure, we interviewed and hired a production manager. She had the experience and skills to do exactly what we needed. We had a production team that was disorganized, failed quality control, missed deadlines, and did a lot of finger-pointing and blame-shifting. No one was taking ownership for any of it. We needed to advance change and we needed help to do it. We saw the qualities in this woman that we needed. I had been there long enough to know that it would be a significant change and we would encounter resistance. I sat down with the CEO and other senior leaders and said, "Are we sure we want to do this? This person is a strong leader and will expect to come in and manage and do what we've hired her to do. There will be pushback, so I need to make sure you are all on board. Our team is not going to like this."

They assured me they were on board, were happy with the hire and were excited to have her on the team. She started as Production Manager on a Monday and people were made aware that she would be responsible for everything in the production area. By the following Monday, our shop supervisor was in the VP's office complaining about the new manager. The VP then called the production team together and asked them how it was going, and they responded that they didn't like her style and she was coming on too strong.

It snowballed from there. The CEO and VP waivered in their decision, bowed to the resistance and did not give the new Production Manager the support she needed. In fact, they undermined her authority, sided with the team that didn't want to change and she failed. She lasted a month or two but ultimately left and the team went back to doing things the way they had always done them. Zero change was advanced in an area in desperate need of it.

3. Know when to fold 'em (be courageous enough to pivot).

In the wisdom of Kenny Rogers and his song, *The Gambler*, part of being a winner at poker is knowing when to walk away, or when to fold your cards and leave the game. This skill is also true of leadership.

   a.   If you have new information that causes you to modify your original assumptions used in making a decision, you may need to change that decision.

   b.   If significant, meaningful data proves that the decision is not having the impact you thought it would, you may need to admit you were wrong and change direction.

Authentic leadership requires vulnerability and a willingness to change direction when necessary, to admit when you were wrong or that information you received was faulty or incomplete.

The current pandemic has given us many examples that relate to this concept. I made decisions in early March 2020 that in hindsight turned out to be wrong. When others were having big reactions to the coronavirus news, I had the mindset of, "We are not changing anything. It is business as usual for us." We had an all-employee meeting on Wednesday, March 11, where I stood in front of our employee group and talked about the future, business as usual, culture, blah blah blah. By Friday of that week, our events had canceled for the remainder of March and a public health order had been issued in our county. By Friday of the following week, we had laid off almost 200 of those same employees whom I had just stood in front of saying it was business as usual. Our situation and position changed rapidly and seemingly overnight, and I had to re-think my approach and recant my speech.

We've seen this play out on the national stage as well in our country, and we've been in desperate need of leaders who can pivot and change direction when the information or facts change rapidly.

When I think back over my career and the mistakes I've made and also witnessed other leaders make, being afraid to fail and, therefore, afraid to make decisions is one of the most common. As leaders, we tend to have fragile egos. We mistakenly believe that being a leader means that you can't or shouldn't fail, and you can't or shouldn't be vulnerable. This mindset actually prevents true leadership from happening and will stifle your ability to advance change.

Many leaders would rather avoid making the tough decisions and instead maintain the status quo than do the hard work involved in the discipline of quality decision-making and taking the risk of bold, courageous decisions.

One of the foundations of authentic leadership is the ability to recognize when you are wrong, when you've made a mistake, and to be able to admit that to your team and change direction.

But it is important to make sure that you are not succumbing to peer pressure or pressure from above or below. The realization that your decision was wrong, or is no longer working for you, should be based on real, measurable outcomes or new information that has been revealed.

Go back to your decision matrix and run through the questions and answers. Are they still true? Has anything changed? Has new information or data come to light? If so, you may need to make a change. If not, hang in there.

If you have real results that have been gathered over a long enough period of time to be meaningful, and your decision is having an impact that is different than what you were looking for or desired, then you may need to make a change.

You need to have the courage and leadership to change your mind and make a different decision. Be courageous enough to pivot. Know when to fold 'em.

Your Turn In The Seat

1. Have you made or been involved in making a challenging or strategic decision? Or perhaps you've watched as the leadership team made one.

2. Was it a quality decision? What tools or analysis were the foundation of that decision? Was there analysis paralysis?

3. Did you encounter resistance? From whom? Customers, vendors or employees?

4. Did the leadership team waiver or courageously stay the course?

5. What could they have done differently throughout this process?

CHAPTER TWELVE

GIVE IT TIME

The final factor in the process of change is time. Time is the simplest of elements and also the most challenging. Remember, **change is the intersection of discernment, discovery and determination.** Determination is the superpower of change. Time is the fuel. Because we get impatient, we need endurance. To advance change, we need to play the long game. As we've been discussing, change does not happen in an instant, or in a meeting, or with one decision. It is a process, and it takes time. The overwhelming nature of change is what causes many, both leaders and their teams, to lose heart.

In order to truly ADVANCE CHANGE, a leader must stand the test of time. This is where your leadership skills will be tested. This is why your company and your team need you. You were hired to keep them focused and motivated, and most importantly, to go the distance.

Change happens when Operational Excellence and Courageous Decisions happen consistently over a prolonged period of time. A new activity/habit/process consistently performed over time equals change.

In the context of advancing change, what do we need to know about time?

1. Time is relative.

2. Go the distance.

1. Time is relative

As leaders, we like answers to our questions. We pride ourselves on knowing things or finding the answers we need, no matter what. But when it comes to the question of, how long will change take? Well, that depends. Because in this case, time is relative.

How long does it take to boil a pot of water? Well, that depends. Boiling a pot of water depends on many factors.

For example, what is the beginning state of the water you are boiling? What is the temperature of the water you are starting with? It matters if you are starting with ice or with hot water, and this will determine how long it will take to get the water to boiling temperature. The same is true with advancing change. Where are you starting from? How far away are you from your goal?

How big is the pot? How much water are you trying to boil? Is it a small pan with one cup of water in it? That will boil fast. Or is it a large stock pot of water? That will take longer. My husband and I hosted a traditional Seafood Boil in May one year and invited a few friends over to introduce this East Coast meal to my Southern Cali friends. A Seafood Boil is when you take a large pot of water, season it with lemons and salt and creole seasoning, and bring it to a boil. Once the water has been boiling for a bit and is infused with all those aromatics, you add potatoes, then corn, sausage, shrimp, clams and mussels. Once everything has cooked, the contents of the pot is dumped out on the table, and everyone dives in. We used one of those propane cookers used to fry turkeys, which is thirty quarts or seven and a half gallons of water. Luckily, I knew from experience (had learned the hard way) and talked to some family members who reminded me, that it could take up to two hours to boil the water. If I hadn't accounted for this time, I would have been in a very difficult situation with my guests sitting around waiting for dinner.

The same is true for your change. What is the scale or size of the change you are advancing?

Finally, how intense is the flame? How high is the heat? If you have the burner on low, it will take much longer than if you turn the knob to high.

When I'm boiling water for pasta or eggs, I always turn to high because I want it to boil as fast as possible. Why not?

In the context of change, how intense is your allocation of resources to make it happen?

All of these examples explain why time is relative and why it is impossible to answer the question of "How long will this change take?"

If we were making brownies, the answer might be a little more exact because we are controlling all the elements. There are exact measurements of all the ingredients, and the instructions on the box tell you the pan size and oven temperature. So the time to make brownies can be easily predicted. Advancing change is much more like boiling water.

How long will your change take? What is the current state? How big is the change? How intense is the flame?

2. Go the distance

Regardless of what your answers were to those questions, to advance change, you must be willing to go the distance.

What does "Go the distance" mean? Well, if you're a boxer, it means you last the entire fight, or fifteen rounds. If you're a major league baseball pitcher, it means your arm holds up for all nine innings. If you're a NASCAR driver in the Daytona 500, it means you don't crash and burn, hit the wall or give up before crossing the finish line after two hundred laps on a two-and-a-half-mile track.

As a leader advancing change, it means you do whatever it takes to stay in the game, to keep standing, to cross the finish line until your change is realized.

One leadership team I worked with had completed an employee survey and received valuable feedback about our culture. The results told us that change was necessary in a few areas, especially in the way we worked with one another. As a result, we developed three tenets of how we were going to change the way we worked with one another. We committed to Kindness and Respect, Open and Consistent Communication, Accountability and Operational Excellence.

We made a big deal of it. At our next culture-building event, after the beer and wine social hour, our staff listened intently about our new culture that we were going to instill through these three tenets. The atmosphere was full of positive energy and hope as the leadership team stepped up in front of the room and signed their name on this life-sized contract with all employees. It was inspiring and impactful. We were high with the possibility of a new way forward, high-fiving and cheers-ing each other after the ceremony.

It was definitely the right first step. But on its own, that signing ceremony did nothing to actually create the change we were committing to.

In the days and weeks after this ceremony, the team waited and watched to see if we meant what we'd promised. Would leadership really behave differently? Would some of us continue to raise our voices and yell when we were frustrated or badger staff about their work? Would we use dismissive and condescending tones? Would we address poor quality of work and hold teams to their deadlines and accountable for the end results? Would we step in and stop bullying and aggressive behavior between the staff in the office?

The three tenets and the ceremony were an important anchor to set the expectations on this new culture we all wanted, but that change could only occur one way—**in the day-to-day** opportunities to courageously exhibit different behavior than we had in the past. Going forward, our choices must line up with these three tenets. Did the change occur? Honestly, I moved on from that role before I was able to witness it, but I know it was a work in progress and something the organization was committed to. But I do know that a change like that was definitely going to require going the distance.

When I was in my early forties, I became a triathlete. To clarify, a sprint triathlete, which means I completed a swim/bike/run course with much shorter distances than the *Iron Man* races you may associate with triathlons. But for me, at that time in my life, the distances may as well have been *Iron Man*. My first event was the *Iron Girl* in Syracuse, New York. I had dreamt of doing a triathlon for close to twenty years, searching for that post-college athletic challenge. I'd bought a couple of books about it, read them and dreamed of doing it, but it stopped there. I was overwhelmed at the thought of attempting something so big, and I was afraid. Afraid I couldn't do it, afraid of trying and just not ready to make that kind of courageous decision and commitment.

I'd had this silver angel ornament hanging from a light pink ribbon on one of the knobs of my dresser ever since I'd received it as a free gift for purchasing something at this cute little gift shop at the Regional Market. A quote from Eleanor Roosevelt was engraved along the edge, "You must do the thing you think you cannot do." I had been meditating on this quote for a couple of years until one day in February 2009, when I was at a real low point in my personal life, I walked by the ornament again and decided that that's exactly what I needed. I needed to do something I didn't think I could do. Around this same time, there was an article in the Sunday paper discussing the controversy caused by the Iron Girl Triathlon that was coming to Syracuse. Women were offended by the use of the word "Girl" as opposed to "Woman". This is what caught my interest. I was also offended and angry, at first. But the story itself stayed with me and nagged at me every time I walked by that angel ornament. I did some research into the event and wondered if I could do it. I tried to convince friends and my sisters to do it with me, but they were not interested. I made the courageous decision to sign up by myself.

I began my training right away because I knew I needed all the time I could get. I started to ride the stationary bike at the gym for one hour once a week. At the time, I didn't have a lot of extra money, so I researched free swimming pools and found out that our city had a few with lap swim available. I started swimming on Sunday afternoons. When I came out of the locker room after my swim, with wet hair, I felt sixteen again. The run was the easiest leg for me to train because I was already running a 5k. I was not part of a fancy coaching group. My training was very simple. I trained to go the distance. For each leg of the upcoming race, I began to train for slightly longer than the expected time. I swam for thirty minutes. Rode the stationary bike for at least an hour and ran for thirty minutes.

The local triathlon club held training sessions every Wednesday night in the summer. We practiced all three legs of the triathlon. The distances were shorter, but we were able to complete all three sports over a couple of hours. Usually, it was a quarter mile swim, 10-mile bike course and 3.1-mile run. The very first night I went to one of these training sessions, I was very nervous. But when the night was over, I knew I would complete the *Iron Girl*.

Here's the thing. Signing up didn't get me ready or talking about it with my friends or sisters. The training sessions didn't immediately get me in shape. It took time. I was moderately in shape when it came to running, but swimming and biking were new for me, at least as an adult. I had never done those sports as a form of exercise. So I had to account for that beginning state. I was also working full time and could only allocate so many hours per week to my training. The size of the change I needed was quantifiable. I had definite distances. Someone else with a different beginning state, or someone who could devote hours and hours per week might have been ready in a shorter period of time.

It took me five months to train and prepare from when I signed up to the day of the event. Instead of being overwhelmed by the whole event, I broke it down into sections. I trained for each leg. I didn't get caught up in fancy gadgets or spend a lot of money. I trained and prepared to go the distance. I didn't train to win, or to achieve outrageously optimistic times, I trained to finish.

How do you know when your change has been accomplished? I think it depends on what you're doing. If you are boiling water, you know when the water is popping and gurgling at a rolling pace. If you're making brownies, it's when the toothpick or knife comes out of the center clean, without any chocolatey goo on it.

Within our organizations, we know we've achieved the desired change when resistance has stopped, acceptance has occurred, and the new process or initiative has become standard operating procedure or habit: second nature. The team doesn't question it, they don't question you, they just do it. You know you've arrived when you don't even have to chime in as the leader. The team is holding each other accountable to the new way of doing things. So the answer is, you'll know when you know.

Change is not for the faint of heart. It is hard as hell. But I promise you this: It will give you courage and strength and resilience that you didn't know you had.

In order to advance change, you must give it time. You must understand the details relative to the particular change and then go the distance, LEADING your team with focus, motivation and DETERMINATION. After all, it's what we're here for.

Your Turn In The Seat

1. Think of three different examples of change you implemented (or attempted to implement).

2. What were the relevant factors that determined how much time was required? What was the beginning state? How intense was the flame? How big was the change?

3. Did you go the distance? If the answer was yes, how long did it take? How did you know when you crossed the finish line? What were the keys to your success?

4. If not, how long did you make it before you threw in the towel? What was it that caused you to give up?

5. What did you do to keep the team motivated and focused for the duration? What could you have done better?

CHAPTER THIRTEEN

CHANGE IN REAL LIFE

We just finished four chapters on change that included a lot of information and instruction on how to advance it. This chapter is a real-life example of an approach I used to ignite change with a group of long-term employees who had been able to coast for too long and had not been held accountable. I was new to the organization and could see that change was definitely necessary.

I was responsible for a team that had become stuck in old patterns. They were failing quality control and were not efficient or productive on a daily basis. Change was necessary and had been for quite a long time. I had heard rumors that this team was particularly resistant and they were notorious for digging in their heels and refusing to change. They had successfully intimidated their managers to allow them to keep doing their work exactly as they wanted to and had continued on their path of least resistance. Physics had taken over and the team was exactly where they wanted to be. But I was not hired to take the path of least resistance. I was there to LEAD. Period. Not sit in my fancy living room/office and avoid the difficult conversation about change that was necessary.

I scheduled a department meeting and brought pizza and cookies. It never hurts to grease the wheels with food. I began my presentation with a warm-up exercise. I was nervous about this exercise based on the group's reputation of being difficult to deal with. I even had a plan with another colleague to rescue me from the conversation if it went off the rails. Instead, it was incredibly positive.

I gave everyone a sticky note and a pen and then asked three questions. I didn't know this team well, and my idea to start with asking these questions was really a way to find out where they were, what they honestly thought, and was also my way of controlling potential resistance in the meeting itself. I figured I would tease out the negativity and get it out in the open early on so it wouldn't sabotage my meeting. I had them silently write their one-word answers on the sticky note. We took our time. We had people with English as a second language, so they needed some help. We took whatever time they needed to answer.

The three questions I asked were:

1. **What is your favorite thing about your job?**
2. **What do you think others in the organization think about you and this department?**
3. **What do you want others to think about your department?**

After the team was finished writing their answers, I collected their sticky notes, read them aloud and wrote their answers on the easel pad for all to see. I didn't call out individuals on their answers, I let them own up to them if they wanted to and watched the conversation organically progress. Their answers were astounding. Contrary to their reputation, and my biases before holding the meeting, their answers revealed that they possessed incredible pride, had a positive view of the work they did and felt that others in the organization regarded them highly. There was very little negativity in any of the answers or conversation. Here's what their actual responses looked like:

1. What do I like best about my job and what I do? (I love my job because...)
   - Service everyone.
   - Service to the people.
   - Good job.
   - Finishing tasks.
   - Overtime.
   - Making sure I finish.
   - My co-workers make me happy.
   - Let us know we are doing a really good job.
   - Hours.
   - Helping employees.
   - Money.
   - Me gusta que siempre hay enque trabajar ocuparse (I like that there is always work to take care of).
   - Hacer mi trabajo (do my job).
   - Limpieza (cleaning).

2. Our department is _____ . (How do I think other departments view us?)
   - Dedicated.
   - Helpful.
   - Hardworking.
   - Consistent.
   - Hardworking.
   - Polite.
   - Hard workers.
   - Helpful.
   - Hardworking.
   - Hard workers.
   - Good work.
   - Limpieza bueno (good cleaning).

- Que Nuestro trabajo es inportante por la comodidad y el orden de personas (that our work is important to the comfort and order of people).
- Trabajamos en equipo (we work as a team).
- Hard workers.

3. I am_____. (What do I want others to think of me?)
   - Dependable.
   - Demonstrably excellent.
   - Very respectful.
   - Hardworking.
   - We are very helpful to others.
   - They like my help.
   - Trustworthy.
   - Very nice person.
   - Beautiful.
   - Agradable (nice).
   - Lenta (slow? gentle?).
   - Una del equipo (one of the team).

You'll notice that these questions are very similar to the questions we asked ourselves in developing our Elevator Pitch of Leadership (Chapter 2). These three questions zoom in on <u>what you do</u> and what you bring to the organization. Remember, we all want our work to matter. Questions two and three give you a chance to articulate how you view yourself, and how you want others to see you. These three things are very important to all of us. And just like the process we discussed with Operational Excellence, asking these questions, and gathering and discussing the answers will reveal much more than just a linear Q&A. This process was so much more effective than if I'd stood up in front of them, talking at them, and telling them how they should approach their work and how they should act if they want to be respected. The magic lies in the process itself. It is very powerful.

It is a powerful thing to have your people and teams use their own words to describe how they feel about their work, what they value, and how they want to be seen and known by others.

This exercise may seem overly simple, but what it did was give me a starting point for leading them where I needed to go next, which was to have a difficult conversation about changing their daily duties and what we were going to start requiring of them. So again, I let them use their own words.

To initiate the conversation about Change, I wrote on the easel pad, "Change is _____," and then I let them fill in the blank.

They said, change is:

- New.
- Hard.
- Good and bad.
- It is growth.
- A new chapter.
- The way we do things.

Again, I let them set the stage for the conversation with their own words. This allowed them to anchor themselves in the conversation without it being directed <u>at</u> them. Remember in the first chapter on change when we talked about how hard it is for us humans? And how our first instinct is to resist it? Allowing the conversation to evolve by starting with asking them about change gave them a chance to relax a little and feel as if they had some control, which made them more open to the process. Rather than standing up and telling them all the things they were doing wrong, we eased into the realization that Change was necessary in order to align with their answers in the first exercise.

My next slide in this presentation offered a formula for change that was inspired by the Lippitt-Knoster Model for Managing Complex Change that was developed by Dr. Mary Lippitt (1987) and popularized by Dr. Timothy

Knoster (1991). I simplified the complex charts developed by others into one easy-to-understand formula. The premise is that you need all of these elements for change to occur. If any one of these is missing, it can lead to confusion, anxiety, slow or gradual change, frustration and perhaps a fit of false starts.

$$\text{VISION}$$
$$+$$
$$\text{SKILLS}$$
$$+$$
$$\text{INCENTIVES}$$
$$+$$
$$\text{RESOURCES}$$
$$+$$
$$\text{PLAN}$$
$$=$$
CHANGE

I walked through each element together with the team. First, I connected the change I was asking for to the company purpose and its mission, VISION and values. Then, we talked about their SKILLS and experience, and what was in it for them. It was important to gain buy-in by illustrating the INCENTIVES and showing people what they will get out of the change. During this segment, I referred them back to the warm-up exercise and what they had told me in their own words about themselves and their department. Then, I committed the management and leadership to providing the RESOURCES they needed. I paused here and asked them what resources they felt they needed. Where were they lacking? What had they been asking for but were ignored? One of the items that bubbled up was their lack of a decent break room and availability for coffee and water. This was an easy win for leadership. Find something (or several things) that you can give them. Appreciate them.

One of our primary roles as a leader is to make sure that our teams have everything they need to be successful. Leaders remove roadblocks and find resources.

Finally, all of this conversation led us to the PLAN, which was the purpose for the meeting in the first place. This is where I was going to ask them for significant change in <u>how</u> they were going about their daily duties and assignments. I introduced checklists and procedures in order to create disciplines and standards, again, tying it back to their words and what they told me about change.

But wait...even though the meeting had been a tremendous success, in the days and weeks that followed, as these changes were put into daily practice and changes were made to their work routine, there was resistance and negative feedback. We were tested. We could not waiver. For me, as a leader, my effort now was in supporting my managers, who were tempted to waiver and give in to the resistance from their teams. I had to lead them through the courageous decision process. We had made the quality decision, and it was the right one. Now I needed to make sure that the daily choices lined up with that decision. When the team came in at 6 a.m. to clock in and start their shift and were handed their new clipboard with the QC checklist along with the changes we had made to their routine, we had to <u>choose</u> to stick with the plan.

When these difficult situations presented themselves, the approach that I had taken in the meeting paid off, and the investment in the conversation gave all of us an anchoring place to return to.

For example, when I heard complaints or encountered resistance from the team, I said things like:

"Remember when you said in that meeting that change is hard? It's not supposed to be easy."

"Remember when you said you like to do a good job? These new processes will ensure that."

"Remember when you said you wanted everyone to have a fair workload? This new way of working will accomplish that."

I had a word cloud made of all those answers to their three questions at the beginning of the meeting and had three posters printed to hang in their breakroom. These served as anchors to remind them of their own words. Not mine, not corporate buzzwords or slogans, but words they had ownership of. It's hard to find fault with your own words.

Your Turn In The Seat

FACILITATING CHANGE: TEAM EXERCISE

Do you have a department or team that sounds familiar to this crew? Try this. Schedule a meeting. Bring food. Hand out sticky notes and pens. Then start the conversation by asking them questions. Let them begin the process of change using their own words. You can use these three questions or tailor them to fit your needs. Collect the sticky notes and read them out loud. Using anonymity, create a master list or word cloud.

1. What is your favorite thing about your job? (What makes you feel satisfied, proud and like you put in a good day's work?)
2. What do you think are your top skills? What do you do best? What is unique about you?
3. What do you think others in the organization think about you and this department?
4. What do you want others to think about your department?

Then, walk them through the FORMULA FOR CHANGE and make sure you address each element and let them know clearly how it is going to work.

When the meeting is over and you all high-five and eat cookies, remember that just because you had a good meeting, change hasn't actually occurred yet. You need to make the CHOICES every day that align with your DECISION to change, and over TIME you will achieve the change you need.

Headlines

✓ Change is the intersection of discernment, discovery and determination.

✓ A culture of **OPERATIONAL EXCELLENCE** will give you the discipline to uncover and uproot weeds that have the potential to choke the life out of your organization.

✓ It is the **COURAGEOUS DECISIONS** we make that determine whether we will remain comfortably at rest on our current path, or whether we will allow the force of change to do its work.

✓ In order to Advance Change, you must give it **TIME**. As a leader, you do whatever it takes to go the distance, to stay in the game, to keep standing, to cross the finish line until your change is realized.

✓ Advancing Change is hard. There is no easy answer or way out. However, a culture of Operational Excellence, Courageous Decisions and Time will ADVANCE CHANGE in you, your teams, and your organization. It's worth it.

CHAPTER FOURTEEN

BONUS—WHAT THE WORLD NEEDS NOW

A karaoke-loving shower singer, I usually have a rolodex of songs queued up in my head that can be triggered at any time with just a word. Lately, I've had that old Jackie DeShannon classic playing, "What the world needs now is love, sweet love, It's the only thing that there's just too little of."

But I can't help thinking that what the world really needs right now, more than anything, more than love, or thoughts and prayers, or good deeds, is leadership. Authentic leadership.

We have a serious leadership crisis in our country, in politics, in public health, in corporate America, in faith and religion, and in all of our civic departments and local governments. We need leadership in addressing racial injustice, the homelessness crisis, the pandemic, and gun control.

HOW CAN LEADERSHIP BE MORE IMPORTANT THAN LOVE?

Love is the only thing. Love wins. Love rules. I agree with you 110%. I do believe that love can be world-changing and life-altering, and it's necessary. But we need leadership, and we need it desperately.

DON'T WE ALREADY HAVE LEADERS?

We recently elected new leaders. We have CEOs and Presidents, Mayors and Commissioners, and others in positions of power. We have people with leadership titles, but leadership is so much more than a title.

Being a leader is more than the position you hold, the title you have, the degree you've earned, the money you make, the size of your company, or the size of the department or team that you manage. Being a leader is so much more than appearances, elections, political positions, fancy corner offices, or impressive titles and salaries. In Chapter 2, we spent some time on the definition of leadership and what it means to us.

Most of this book is devoted to leadership in the context of business and our careers. In this bonus chapter, I want to take a little detour from that and talk about the importance of leadership in our world, in our country, cities and towns, and in our culture.

Regardless of how you or I define leadership, at the end of the day, I'm not interested in even my own definition, fancy buzzwords, or corporate BS. When it comes to authentic leadership, I know it when I see it, and you probably do too. I am more interested in what leadership looks like on a daily basis in the trenches. Who is providing leadership when we are faced with a worldwide pandemic, or the crisis of citizens of our own country being murdered on the streets by people who are supposed to protect them or dying from homelessness or an opioid addiction? I am interested in leadership when we have insurgents storming our Capitol building. I am more interested in leadership when our economy is crashing, and people need relief and financial support.

WHAT DOES LEADERSHIP DO FOR US?

There are four primary things that leadership gives us. Leadership provides:

- **Vision.**
- **Unity.**

- **Inspiration.**
- **Strength.**

Leadership provides **Vision**. Proverbs 29:18, a scripture in the Bible, says that "Where there is no vision, the people perish." Vision allows us to see what is possible and where we need to go. It also gives us a plan and a path on how to get there. Leaders have vision about where we need to go, and can guide us on how to get there. They can tell us what the map looks like, what the roadmap is and what directions we need to follow.

We need vision as a collective group, because as individuals, we are pulled in too many different directions. We all have different priorities, needs, crises and egos. We all have different resources available to us, including privileges and abilities, whether they are physical or intellectual or otherwise. We are all caught up in the weeds of our own life. So much so that we need someone who can see above and outside all of that and give us a vision.

We need someone who can help us imagine a different future than the one we've been handed, and not just imagine it, but lead us on the path to get there.

Leadership provides **Unity** and brings people together around a common goal in spite of all the differences and conflict. We witness a lot of ugliness on the news and in social media and sometimes even within our own friend group or family.

I believe that the majority of people are good and that we all want the same things. One of my credos in life, which I included at the beginning of my book, *Chasing the Merry-Go-Round,* is this: Home is a place all of us want to be. We all want to have our corner of the world, surrounded by people who know us, accept us, love us; a place where we are safe, warm, fed; a place where we have enough, where we are enough. This is all there is. I also believe that how we care for those who need help has an everlasting impact, and that if we can help people meet the basic needs of their spirit, soul and body, it allows them the ability to keep their own corner of the world, their home, safe and prosperous for them and their family. This is all there is.

At our core, as human beings, that is what we all want. And if we all want the same thing, I believe that we can rally around that, even though we may all have different ideas on how to get there. When I use the word unity, I'm not implying that we all have to follow the same path. There is not one path for everyone. Unity in the context of being a leader is someone who can rise up and remind us that even though we disagree on different things, we all want many of the same things. We all want a home. We all want to have enough. We all want our corner of the world. We need someone who can help us unite around that idea when we're pulled in all these different directions.

Leadership provides **Inspiration**. We are confronted with bad news on a daily basis. Our access to 24/7 news and the sensational nature of it, the way some of our so-called leaders are behaving and the devastating stories that are thrust in our face, can be overwhelming and discouraging. Why haven't we made more progress in the areas of social justice? Why are people dying on the streets, unsheltered, hungry or addicted? Why can't we solve these issues that plague us?

We can watch videos on YouTube that make us feel like we're on that street, watching it happen. It's devastating and we feel helpless. We feel like we're standing by, silently watching these horrible things unfold before our eyes. We wonder why we can't do anything to stop it. Perhaps we can't worry about what is happening on a national scale because we lost our job and are consumed with trying to make our next mortgage payment so our family doesn't end up sleeping in the car, or maybe we're trying to figure out how to buy groceries or find health insurance because our four-year-old was just diagnosed with leukemia.

We need inspiration from our leaders to remind us of who we are, what we're capable of, and that we can all impact and change the world.

Finally, authentic leadership gives us **Strength**. It gives us the resolve, the determination, the resilience to stay in it for the long game, to go the distance, to get back up when we fall, to turn away from those things that hold us down and hold us back. Leadership sends a message to our enemies and those who wish us harm. A leader can be strong for us when we're too weak to keep going.

VISION. UNITY. INSPIRATION. STRENGTH.

Those are the reasons we need authentic leadership. But let's get practical. What does it look like? What is an authentic leader? Everything we learned about leadership at the beginning of *Here to LEAD* translates to leadership in this context.

If you are an authentic leader, you are honest, committed, flawed, curious and open. Authentic leadership is also self-aware and not ruled by fear. This is very important with all we are faced with in our world today. We need leaders who are not making decisions out of fear, are comfortable with making mistakes and able to make the tough decisions, all while remaining vulnerable and transparent. Someone who is willing to be wrong or change their mind when faced with new information. We need more vulnerability and transparency in our leaders, not perfection. Authentic leaders say things like:

"I screwed up. Here's where I went wrong last week. I apologize. I own it. I want to move forward. And here's what I'm going to do differently."

"I don't know the right answer at this time but I'm putting all my resources into figuring it out."

"I've changed my position on that topic. I know what I said before, but I have new information that has changed my mind."

"I was wrong."

Authentic leaders are collaborative, which means they are willing to rely on the expertise of others. They don't need to be the one with all the answers. It's impossible for one human being to know everything, and that's okay. They just need to be able to find the answers or the people who have them and build strong teams around them. And also hold those teams accountable, which is often a missing piece.

An authentic leader is capable. They need to have the skill set for whatever leadership position they're in. If it's business, they need to have business acumen. They need to be educated in their area of expertise, trained, hardworking and focused. They need to be capable of doing the job they're doing.

Finally, an authentic leader is strong, decisive, accountable, willing to make the tough decisions and to have the tough conversations. When we're looking for a leader, we need to look for these attributes. Can this person provide vision and unity, inspiration and strength? Does the person I'm voting for or hiring or following provide these things? Are they able to provide vision unity, inspiration and strength? Are they authentic? Are they vulnerable enough to be transparent, open and honest, willing to make mistakes and be imperfect? Are they willing to collaborate? Are they willing to hold their teams and themselves accountable? Are they capable? Do they have the capability to do the job we're expecting them to do? Are they strong enough?

We need to consider all these things when we're deciding who to elect, who to hire, who to follow and who we allow to fill the leadership roles in our life.

PART FOUR

Drive Results

A business, like an automobile, has to be driven, in order to get results.

—B.C. FORBES

CHAPTER FIFTEEN

ARE YOU IN THE DRIVER'S SEAT?

Driving Results is the fourth anchor of *Here to LEAD*. We have developed our elevator pitch and have a better understanding of who we are as a leader. We've learned what it takes to execute strategy and advance change. You might think that now that we've spent that significant time and energy on those important things that the hard work is done and now the results, the outcomes and the goals we were trying to achieve, will come naturally, as a by-product of all that effort and intention. Unfortunately, there is still work to do.

DRIVING RESULTS: WHAT IS IT? WHY DO WE NEED IT? HOW DO WE DO IT?

One definition of the word "drive" is "to propel or carry along by force in a specified direction." For our purposes, that means to cause and guide the movement of your team, your department or your organization, depending on where you are in the leadership team. Driving results takes work. Even if you have all the leadership skills and have mastered the execution of strategy and advancing change, you will still need some tools to make sure you are driving results. It doesn't happen automatically. Results are not a given.

Organizations and leadership teams tend to have lack of attention or lack of focus, especially in a startup or entrepreneurial company or culture. We talked about this in the Executing Strategy section. Entrepreneur CEOs are idea people. That's what they do. They have ideas. Which is fine, as long as they have leaders on their team who can take the wheel and keep driving. Often, though, projects are launched, and then the leadership moves on to the next great idea. People get bored. They are addicted to and need adrenaline so there are many projects started. It's always exciting at the beginning. There's a kick-off meeting, but then as time moves on, people lose focus, they lose the will to maintain, and no one is reminding them of their commitments.

You may spend a significant amount of time and money getting your car ready to drive with brand new tires, an oil change, clean filters in place and new brakes installed. You've washed it, waxed it, cleaned the windows inside and out, vacuumed up all the dried mud, French fries and cookie crumbs and filled the gas tank. The car is ready to go. But...you still have to drive it. You have to keep your hands on the wheel. The thing about cars is that they weigh more than four thousand pounds and carry a tremendous amount of momentum, force and potential. Most importantly, no matter what you've done to prepare them, they are designed to be actively driven.

If you're driving your car and you take your hand off the wheel or foot off the gas, the car may coast and go straight for a period of time; we've all tried it, but eventually, the road you're on will curve or fork, or there will be something in the road you need to avoid, whether it's another car or maybe even an animal. My niece was driving her Ruby (Kia Spectra) on a busy highway one Saturday and the car in front of her had a mattress strapped to the roof. The mattress became loose and then airborne, at 65 mph, and slammed into my niece's little car with full force. Luckily, she was a good driver and had her hands on the wheel, so she was able to negotiate the impact and pull to the side of the road. While there was minor damage to her car, thankfully, she was unhurt. My niece was skilled enough and experienced enough to not panic. But if she hadn't been in control of her car, if she hadn't been driving and just left the car to its own devices, the situation would have been much worse. If you don't have your hand on the wheel when something unexpected happens, the car will crash, go off the road, or perhaps cross the center line into oncoming traffic.

Our staff and teams need someone in the driver's seat. They need someone who is skilled, experienced, strong, willing to drive when it is clear and sunny, when it is dark and rainy, and when you are in slow-moving traffic. I lived in San Diego for a few years and experienced "traffic" like I'd never experienced before, and it takes some special skills. If you live in and around a major city, you understand that "traffic" is a verb, a noun and a cliché. It is the thing that determines whether or not you'll take a job in a certain area, or what time to make dinner reservations or whether or not it is worth it to go to the beach. You need to navigate the freeway with finesse and skill, and even a little luck in order to survive it. You also need a kick-ass playlist, audiobook or podcasts to listen to.

Our teams need someone who knows how to swerve, slow down or speed up, depending on the conditions you encounter. They need a leader. Your leadership skills, just like driving skills, and just like everything else we've covered throughout this book, get better with experience and time in the seat.

You could be the best driver in your household and among all your friends. Perhaps you pride yourself on your ability to negotiate all kinds of driving conditions. Maybe you're one of those people who brags about driving faster than the speed limit and about all the tickets you've racked up over the years... doesn't matter. You still need to remain in control of the vehicle.

I grew up and have spent most of my life in the Northeast, so I had to learn how to drive on snowy, icy roads in whiteout conditions, freezing temperatures and blinding snowstorms. If you're familiar with that cliché, you know what it's like to be at the windshield, straining to see into a black abyss with tiny white dots bombarding your eyes while you fight off falling into a trance. It is scary. But I had some good teachers. My dad taught me that when the temperature is below thirty-two degrees, you need to watch out for black ice. You might not be able to see it, but if the roads are wet and the temperature drops, the pavement will freeze. Traffic and the warmth created from other drivers and their tires on the road will warm up the pavement a little, but you still have to be on the lookout.

My mom taught me that if you're having trouble knowing where the center line is or you're blinded by oncoming headlights, just keep your eye on the white line on the right side of the road and at least you know you won't go into a ditch. I also learned that if you hit a patch of ice and lose control of the car, you turn your steering wheel in the same direction you're spinning, not against it. It is scary, but you get used to it and with time and practice, you develop skills, usually after encountering some of these frightening situations for yourself and coming out the other side with you and your car intact.

As the driver, you need to watch out for the weather and road conditions, but sometimes you need to watch out for other drivers. We've all heard the term backseat driver, right? Those who feel like they have knowledge and information that you need in order to drive the car successfully. As a backseat driver myself, I wholeheartedly believe that sometimes the driver does need my information, but then again, sometimes they don't. The person in the driver's seat is the one who has the control. **As a leader, that is you. You make the decisions. You decide how fast or slow to move, you decide where to turn, you decide when you just need to keep going.**

One summer when I was about ten years old, we were vacationing in the Adirondacks with a group of people, and we went horseback riding. This wasn't something that I did a lot, although I loved horses. We had even owned our own ponies for a few years when I was growing up, but I definitely did not consider myself, then or now, a skilled horse rider.

We were all moseying along pleasantly on our afternoon ride, when my horse got spooked by something and just took off. Suddenly this horse was hell bent on getting back home. She was running as fast as she could and all I could do was hold the reins and try not to slam headfirst into the ground. My saddle became loose and started moving to one side, so I'd scooch it back up to her back and then fall down the other side. I'm sure it would have been a viral video if someone had captured it on a cell phone, but we didn't have those back then. Somehow, I made it back to the stable without falling off or getting dragged behind my horse. I was lucky.

A skilled rider would have been able to pull the reins in, strong and steady, in order to calm the horse and get her to slow down or stop. The reins and the bit in the horse's mouth are what guides, controls and drives them. That day in the Adirondacks, my reins were flying loose, which only made things worse. When I got into this situation, I didn't have the skills or experience to do any of that. And it showed.

This is why your team needs you.

 Projects can sometimes take on a life of their own and move at speeds or in directions that were never intended, and if you don't have your hands on the reins, if you're not guiding the horse and controlling that bit, it will go wherever it feels like.

Also, if others in the organization don't see a leader in the driver's seat, they may try to take your spot or grab the wheel. One day, I was riding in the front of our pickup truck with my sister. She was sixteen and driving, and I was sitting in the middle seat next to her, and I think my mom was to my right. The roads were snowy and she hit a slippery patch. The truck started to veer and I reached over and grabbed the wheel. I panicked and didn't trust her, apparently, to drive us through it. She was a good driver and didn't need my help, but I did it anyway. She got so mad at me and let me know how stupid it was to do that. What I did actually put us in more danger. I learned a valuable lesson that day. Someone else grabbing the wheel of the car you're driving is dangerous and not something you should allow to happen.

IF WE DON'T DRIVE, SOMEONE OR SOMETHING ELSE WILL.

I was working for a company that had an exciting opportunity to expand our products in a national chain of luxury retail stores. It was something we had worked toward for a long time and a great win for our business. This new sales channel was an execution of our strategy. I was a senior finance leader, but I wasn't driving this onboarding experience. I witnessed it from a distance. I had previous experience working with this chain and a few other similar ones. I knew there were going to be bumps in the road and that the driving conditions were going to be unfamiliar to this group because they had never done business with a large chain like this. Historically, our company did business mostly with independent retailers, who have their own set of unique characteristics, challenges and benefits. Large, national chains, especially in the luxury sector, were a unique type of customer. They are used to operating at a different level with different expectations. We would need EDI (electronic data interchange) capability, and we would need to provide product spec sheets with details that had to be exact, and we would need to invoice them a certain way, and ship our products according to their instructions. I knew what to look for and I had some experience navigating the icy patches and the spinouts.

As I watched this opportunity unfold at my company, I witnessed all the different departments working so hard to make it happen, from merchandising to sales to operations, production and finance. Everyone was working hard to prepare for this new customer and this new sales channel. But...I saw an empty driver's seat and I was nervous. Instead of just grabbing the wheel and jerking it like I had done with my sister, I went to my boss and asked if I could take the wheel and form a cross-departmental team that could work together to make this happen. I explained my experience and the skills I was sure were necessary in this situation. My boss was all for it. He let me take the wheel and drive.

That doesn't mean I did all the work, or that I knew everything. I didn't. I had a great team that knew the details in their areas of expertise and all I had to do was drive. I could provide insight and experience, tell them what to expect up the road and around the corner and what flying mattresses we needed to avoid. We were ultimately successful. But if we hadn't had a driver in place, I'm not sure how it would have worked out. I'm sure the customer would have still come onboard, but there might have been a few crashes and a few off-road adventures along the way.

Hopefully, I've convinced you how important it is to DRIVE your team, your projects and your organization.

 Yes, leadership development is important, and so is executing strategy and advancing change. These are all critical skills that you need to have in place. But you can't do all that and then take your hands off the wheel.

I've seen this over and over again in organizations I've been in, where the leaders have cast the vision, set the strategy, launched the right projects in the right direction, and then took their hands off the wheel, and moved on to the next thing. And when that happens, guess what else happens most of the time? The car never gets to where it was intended to go.

Now that we've established that as leaders we need to drive, let's talk about why results are important.

WHY ARE RESULTS, OUTCOMES AND THE IMPACT OF WHAT WE'RE DOING SO IMPORTANT?

Everyone in your organization wants their work to matter. They want to know and need to know that showing up, day after day, meant something to you, to the organization, and to others. We all want to be successful, to do a good job. It is hard-wired in us as humans. It doesn't matter if your job is to sweep the floors, enter invoices, or pack boxes; we all have this need, not just the people in positions that we've come to associate with success. In our American capitalist culture, we mistakenly assume that people with less visible or lower paid jobs don't care about their work. That's not true. That example I gave you in the last chapter about advancing change was with a housekeeping department. Remember all the things they said about the pride they had in their team and their jobs and how they wanted to be viewed by other people? That example was a department that was responsible for cleaning venues. Maslow's hierarchy of needs talks about the human need of esteem. We all possess it. We all want respect from others and from ourselves, **and we all have a need for achievement.**

Remember, too, the analogy of the fancy living room. As leaders, we are not here to sit still and look pretty. We are here to get stuff done. **We need to cross the finish line, or else what was the point of it all?**

If we don't grow top-line revenue, or customer base, or increase market share, brand awareness, reduce expenses, whatever the thing is that you identified as the right goal for your organization, if we don't actually achieve that, then what was it all for? We'd be better off just letting our business keep doing what it's doing, save ourselves time and money, let the reins fly, hold on for dear life and pray that we survive. Because if you're not intentionally driving results, that is what's already happening in your organization. Your cars are all over the place. Your people are on their horses, bouncing and falling off the saddle and holding on for dear life. If your team sees projects continuously flounder without a driver, they will lose interest. They'll lose motivation. They'll lose faith that the goals that you've put in front of them are even possible.

We've established what it means to drive results and why we need it. But as you know, with *Here to LEAD*, we are all about the How. How do we do it? What does it mean to drive in this context?

How do we keep our hands on the wheel, our car on the road and moving in the right direction?

The good news is, driving results is as easy as our ABCs.

THE ABCS OF DRIVING RESULTS

1. **A**ssign.
2. **B**eware.
3. **C**ommunicate.

Your Turn In The Seat

1. Think of a time when you were either leading or part of a project and the driver's seat was empty. What was the project? Was there ever a driver in the seat? Or did you have one and perhaps they became distracted or pulled off to another project? Perhaps there were too many backseat drivers who tried to grab the wheel. Maybe you crashed and burned. Take some time to think about this in the context of the chapter you just read.

2. For the project above, did you or your team arrive where you wanted to go? Did you get the results you were looking for? What was the end result? Did you crash and burn? Go off road? Run out of gas?

3. What do you think could have been done differently? Knowing what you know now, what would you do differently?

CHAPTER SIXTEEN

ASSIGN

When it comes to driving results, we need to first make sure the assignments are in place. We're all familiar with the corporate buzz and culture of SMART goals. Whatever we set out to do should be specific, measurable, achievable, realistic, time bound. Yeah, yeah, yeah, we got it. We have project-management certifications and smart, flashy project-management software.

We are fairly good at assigning owners to projects, most of the time, and we're pretty good about assigning a due date. So what's the problem?

Where this activity of driving results typically falls short is in thoroughly defining and assigning where we will see the impact of our change and understanding how we will measure it. We need a roadmap.

I'm old-school when it comes to navigating road trips. I pride myself on my map reading skills and navigational tools. I love reading maps. I know it sounds odd, but it's true. Especially in this world of MapQuest and Google Maps and apps that help you get where you're going. I used to check Waze or the traffic app at the end of the day to see if the 52 was red or if I should take the 15, and if they were all red, I would just go work out in the gym for an hour, waiting until the roads changed color before I went home. If you've ever used one of these traffic apps around a big city, you know what I'm talking about.

So I do embrace technology. I'm not a complete Luddite. But I also embrace old-school geography and understanding basic direction and knowing whether I am traveling north or west and what major cities I am going to pass through. A few years ago, I was talking to someone on my team and asked him what he had planned for the weekend. He said he was taking a trip from Boston to DC. "Oh, I love DC," I said. "My nephew's at Howard University right now. How are you getting there?" I was curious if he was going to drive or fly. I had just flown from Boston to DC, and it was easy and inexpensive, so I was curious and interested and excited. He said, "We're driving."

"Oh, yeah? What route are you taking?" I got even more excited and asked if he was going to take 95 all the way, and wanted to share with him my lessons learned about timing and traffic and the best way to navigate through New York City and Connecticut and which bridge to take, and he just stood there staring at me silently, eyes wide, mouth open. He finally shrugged his shoulders and said, "Uh, I was just going to put it in my phone."

"Oh," I said, disappointed. No doubt he was bewildered as to why I had asked so many darn questions and what the big deal was and why I was so excited over his road trip. It was also clear to me that he hadn't thought through any of these details. He was just going to get in the car with his girlfriend, plug the address into his app, and take for granted that it would work out and he would get there. I know he's not alone or unusual. That's how a lot of people do it today.

I need more of a road map than that. I do use my navigation system in my car, and I do use Google Maps to get me where I'm going, but for a serious road trip, I always like to know where and how I'm going to get there. I need to know if I'm going north or if I'm going south. I need to know the major highways I'm going to take. What major cities will I be going through? Are there any dicey or tricky parts that I need to be aware of? Are there any bodies of water? How many miles is it? And that, of course, will help me understand how long it's going to take me. Is it a one-day trip or a two-day trip? Is it suitable for a weekend, or do I need to take Monday off?

My family used to take a beach vacation to Delaware every year, but in the past few years, we've migrated to the Outer Banks in North Carolina. I took it upon myself to send detailed directions to everyone. I would write them up old-school in a Word document, like this:

81 South through Binghamton to Clarks Summit, PA (Exit 194) to PA turnpike (476S). Stay on PA turnpike to Exit 20 (old exit 25A) (476S). Follow 476S to 95 S (Chester/Philadelphia) toward Wilmington to exit 11, take 495 S (beltway around Wilmington). 495 S will merge back into 95S. From 95S take exit 4A to Rte 1 S – Christiana to Dover – Be careful here and watch the signs, it gets confusing. Stay on 1S, you may see signs for 13S and 113S. Stay on this route, take no turns. You are going to Dover, to Milford and then to Rehoboth Beach. Right before you get into the town of Milford, you will bear to your left and follow signs for 1S to Rehoboth Beach. Take 1S and stay on this road through the town of Lewes to Rehoboth Beach.

Chronological order of cities:

1. *Syracuse*
2. *Binghamton*
3. *Philadelphia*
4. *Wilmington*
5. *Dover*
6. *Milford*
7. *Rehoboth*

I took a lot of heat for this. Now I can see that it may have been slightly overly detailed and understand why my siblings made fun of me. What I was really trying to do was to give them all the information that I like to know for myself. This is the kind of detail that I like to know even if I am using technology. You never know if you're going to lose WiFi or cell coverage, or when your car's satellite won't update your route because of tall buildings, right? That actually happened to me once in the middle of midtown Manhattan, when I was trying to use my Garmin, one of the original GPS products that you plugged into your cigarette lighter, and when surrounded by all those tall buildings it wouldn't work. I've been in those crisis situations and details like this helped me through.

Are you a roadmap person or a fly-by-the-seat-of-your pants person? Are you like that guy who was just going to get in the car with his girlfriend, punch the address into his phone, and head out on a Friday afternoon to DC? Or, are you more of a detailed person like me who wants to know the cities you're going to travel through and whether you're going north or south? The point of this question is to uncover a potential blind spot that you may have. If you know you are a fly-by-the-seat-of-your-pants person, if you know that about yourself and that's your personality, then you need to make sure that you pause before a project is launched and take the time to go through these questions. Uncover your own blind spot before someone else does it for you. That's never fun.

When we talk about driving results in our organizations, in our teams, and in our departments, we need that same kind of detail. The first thing we need to make sure is in place are the assignments, and that's how we get that detail. **We know this intellectually, and yet we often neglect this most important part of the trip.**

Even though we all know that our projects and goals should be specific, measurable, with a due date, we still need to know all the details. We need to talk about it, spend some time on it, and flesh it out before we just excitedly jump in our car and hit the road. Before we start the project, we need to ask ourselves some detailed questions and listen to the answers.

Let's talk it through. There are five assignments that we need to make when launching a project or initiative that is going to execute strategy and advance change. Here they are:

1. <u>**What**</u> **are you going to do?**
2. <u>**Who**</u> **will do it?**
3. <u>**When**</u> **will we be done?**
4. <u>**Why?**</u> **What is your why? Or the impact that you're hoping for?**
5. <u>**How**</u> **will we measure it?**

What, who, when, why, and how. Those are the five assignments. Those are the details we need to talk through before we launch an initiative or project. Otherwise, we will not drive results.

1. What are you going to do?

I recently planned a major road trip. My husband and I moved from the West Coast to the East Coast and drove our car, full of items that were too precious for the moving truck, including our forty-lb. dog. Our goal for this trip, for this mission, was to not only get from point A to point B but to also have an adventure along the way. What that meant to us was mapping out a route that would take us through states and cities and areas that we hadn't been before and were really interested in. We had no interest in driving straight through in a couple of days and sleeping in our car. So, the "<u>what</u>" was to drive from the West Coast to the East Coast, and to have fun doing it. The first step for us in planning this trip was to sit down together and talk about what this looked like to each of us and to define our <u>what</u>. What was it that we are trying to do? What did we want out of it? We agreed that we needed to get from point A to point B, and discussed the experience we wanted to have while doing it.

In the context of business, perhaps you are trying to grow your customer base and you've determined through the work you've done around executing strategy that this is one of your top three priorities in your business. You know it is the right thing to do, and you've done the Red Light Green Light decision matrix on a project that will drive customer base. You've partnered with an affiliate who's going to give you access to their membership and allow you to make an offer to draw them in and buy from you. This initiative checked all the boxes on the decision matrix, and so now you are ready to launch the project. That is your <u>what</u>.

When you sit down to have this planning session to make all these assignments, it may seem redundant because you've already gone through all this work identifying the project and determining that it is the right thing to do. That's why you're having the conversation in the first place. But it doesn't hurt to restate, to reclarify, redefine, put it down on paper, type it into the laptop, put it up on the white board, that this is your <u>what</u>. Remind everybody in the room that this is what you're trying to do because it will also set the context for answering the next four questions, which is important.

2. Who is going to do it?

Assigning the people and resources to your project can seem like an easy exercise, but often we don't spend enough time fully thinking this through. You may have the perfect person in mind for owning this project, but have you stopped to consider if they have the bandwidth to successfully take on another project? Make sure that you've considered this, or you will set yourself up for failure. Are you assigning the person who never says no or never gives any pushback? They're really good at what they do, and you know they have the skills, but do they have the time? Do they actually have the time? Or do they have too much on their plate?

In the section on executing strategy, we learned how damaging it can be to overload people who also have day jobs. So make sure you're not backsliding and forgetting everything we've already learned up to this point. If you've followed all the other advice so far, you should have already considered these things. Assuming that you did, then assign the project owner and then also assign the team that's going to support the project owner.

Who is doing the driving on the first leg? Who's driving from here to Tucson? Who's driving from Tucson to San Antonio? Who's going to drive home? Who's going to do the final stretch? When are you going to take breaks and sleep? And how are you going to work it all in?

Who's going to be the point of contact for the affiliate that you're partnering with to grow customer base? Who's going to provide the reporting? Who's on the team with the project owner? Do you have someone from IT, marketing or customer retention? Often, we spend the least amount of time on this one because we think it's a no-brainer. Or we assign a project owner just to put a name next to it so we can move on. We're proud of ourselves and a little smug, we want to check the box and move on. I would encourage you to spend some time here talking through who will do what in a realistic and honest way and listen to the feedback, and also pay attention to the nonverbal feedback coming from your team. If you're assigning people to a project and they're rolling their eyes, kicking each other under the table, passing notes, sighing loudly, pay attention to that. Don't ignore it. Dig a little deeper. Ask some questions. Can they legitimately take on what you're asking and expecting them to do? Can they drive this project to the result you want? It is better for you to find this out in the planning stages than halfway through the project, when it's failing. As the leader, this is your responsibility. It is not to simply put a name next to a project so you can play the blame game and shift responsibility when the project doesn't get completed. Even if you do assign the project owner, the ultimate responsibility ends with you. As a leader, you're always on the hook. So why not get it right in the beginning? Why not get it right the first time?

3. When will you get where you are going?

As my husband and I planned our trip to the East Coast, we talked about timing. We looked at an old-school map first and laid it out on the table. We figured out a tentative route of where we wanted to go, and then he determined the distances between the cities using MapQuest.

We also talked about how much we're comfortable driving at one stretch. We are not those people who pride themselves on driving straight through no matter what, or getting up in the middle of the night to start a journey. I have a brother like this, and when we go on our beach vacation, he gets his family up at 3:00 in the morning, they all pile in the car, and they drive for twelve hours straight. That is not me; that is not my husband. We don't do that unless we absolutely have to, like if somebody's life depends on it. For us, a four- to six-hour day is a light day. Eight hours for us is the sweet spot. That's our standard where we feel like we've made some good progress, but we also have some energy left when we get there. Eleven to twelve hours is a long day, and we do those every once in a while. Remember, our <u>what</u> was to make the drive but also to explore and have fun while we're doing it. If we plan to drive twelve hours every day, we will not have the energy to go out at night and sample food and drinks around town or go on a hike or take pics with aliens in Roswell, New Mexico, or stand on the corner in Winslow, Arizona. We've done both of those things on previous road trips. We know this about ourselves, and we make it part of the planning process. Not that we don't have some grueling twelve-hour days. We do. But we don't have too many, and we plan them strategically before cities that are only a pit stop, where we have no interest in exploring and will just be crashing at the hotel. Those are the days when we do the long drives.

In order to successfully drive results, you need to have some honest conversations about how long it will take you to achieve the desired customer base growth you're looking for. If you look at the numbers and complete the analysis, how many accounts are you going to be exposed to through this new partner? How many will be presented with your offer? What is your typical close rate on an offer? Use the information that you have in your history and your experience to predict how long it's going to take you to get there. **This is not the time to assume your close rate will magically increase or to use unrealistic and aspirational numbers.** If your expectations are unattainable and unrealistic, guess what? You will never arrive. You will never see results.

Asking your team to grow a customer base by 20% in one year when it has never happened before, and won't this time, unless the planets align or the moon is in Aquarius, is unrealistic. It's like planning to drive from the

West Coast to the East Coast in eight hours. It's physically impossible, at least with the driving technology we have today.

It is impossible to drive three thousand miles in eight hours. It is impossible to grow your customer base by 20% unless you acquire a competitor, which isn't in the plans. Use your actual historical numbers.

This is the time in the process where you want to be as realistic as possible. You've already teased out the great ideas, you've done the brainstorming and the dreaming, and now you're in the tactical stage of getting it done. And this is where you have to be the most realistic, the most honest, and have the most realistic expectations. So use your actual numbers. Use your history. Resist the urge to predict that this group of customers is going to behave differently from any other group you've marketed to.

I know from experience that it is easy to get excited about the potential of a new project and to inflate expectations. We also want to motivate people. We want to dangle the carrot out there. We want to ask our people to stretch. We want to have big, hairy, audacious goals. All of those are valid reasons; however, in this phase of planning, when you're getting down to the tactical nitty gritty of how you're going to do it, you've got to be very honest or you're only fooling yourself, and you won't get the desired result you want. It's only going to lead to frustration and a failed mission. If you're driving four hundred miles, it is going to take you six hours. Period. End of story. That's it.

4. Why are we doing this?

In order to successfully drive results, you must assign the <u>why</u>. Why are you launching this project? What exactly are you trying to do? The right answer is not to drive more revenue or profits. That is the high-level strategy. The question you're asking at this part of the process is <u>why</u> are we doing this particular project? Why are we creating this initiative? What is the specific result we are looking for? And again, I know you're thinking this is overkill, but stay with me. Is the plan to drive from San Diego to Syracuse? Or is the plan to drive from San Diego to Atlanta? You can't be as general as, "Oh, we're driving to the East Coast." The East Coast spans over two thousand miles. So you need a specific target destination or else how will you know when you get there? So the answer you're looking for sounds something like this: We are launching a partnership with this affiliate marketer in order to increase customer base by 5% annually.

Drill down and set your target. Be specific about it. This is important because it plays into answering the next question.

5. How will we measure it?

The final element that needs to be assigned in order to drive results is <u>how</u>. Not as in, how we are going to do it? You've already figured that out. You already know that you are driving instead of flying or taking the train. The project itself is the how. Instead, it is how will you measure results? This is the one we get hung up on and oftentimes fail to spend enough time talking about before the project gets started. How will we know if results are being achieved? How will we know if our project is successful? The way we know whether or not we're being successful is to define, in advance, how we're going to measure results. Then make sure the data we need is available, and finally, set mileposts along the way.

    a.   What is the measurement?

    b.   Is the data available?

    c.   What are the mileposts we'll need along the way to stay on course?

a. What is the measurement?

Since we've already said that we want to grow customer base, wouldn't it make sense to measure results with customer base? What more do we need to know?

The problem is that often we don't spend time talking about this because we take for granted that we will know whether or not it's working. *We're smart people. We're leaders. We've got a handle on our business. We will know if customer base is growing.*

The reality is, if you don't intentionally determine <u>how</u> you will measure results in a way that is clear and manageable, you will not achieve the results you need.

You won't know if your project is successful or not. And if that's the case, then what is the point of it all? Also, if you don't pursue buy-in and clarity up front, you will find yourself in disagreement down the road about whether or not the project is working. You will, trust me. Here's an example of what I'm talking about:

How do you define a customer? In your company and in this context, is a customer one who makes a one-time purchase or is it a one-time purchase over a certain dollar amount, or is a customer someone who buys two to three times in an annual cycle? How does your system count customers? How is your customer retention report calculating customer count? Or do we define a customer as someone who joins our subscription or membership club? Don't assume that everyone is on the same page about this. Tease it out. Decide in advance how you intend to measure what a customer is. If you don't intentionally determine how you will count a customer, you will never know if your project is successful. Then what is the point?

Also, do you mean that you are measuring overall customer base growth, which is a net number of gains and losses, or are you measuring new customers added specifically by this endeavor? Can you attribute all sales activity to this affiliate? I'm sure you, like me, have been part of organizations where marketing attribution is a nightmare, especially if you have multiple campaigns and projects going on at the same time. I'm not in the marketing department and I do not wish to speak ill of my marketing friends. I love the marketing department. They've taught me so much about marketing that I didn't know. Plus, they are the coolest department. They're always having fun. They get to put on the trendy events. They have the highly visible projects, and they have all the flashy graphics and artwork. They can come to work with purple hair or orange pants and nobody cares. They're the fun department. I love hanging out with them. But you have to make sure that when there are multiple marketing projects and campaigns going on that we are only attributing one effort to each customer acquisition. You can't have multiple projects claiming the same customer, claiming that their project was the one that drove that customer. **Otherwise, you're never going to know which project is successful, which one you need to pull the plug on or which one you need to invest more dollars in.** You've got to figure this out ahead of time.

The reason I'm so passionate about this is because I've seen it happen time and time again. You all get started on a project and there is always one person who is more invested than everyone else, usually the one who had the idea and whose pet project it is. But when you start to have honest conversations about the results, and then a report in the monthly meeting shows that customer base is flat, an icy chill suddenly fills the room and everyone is afraid to speak.

At the beginning of the project, you all agreed that you were going to measure it by overall total customer base. But when the latest report says customer base is flat, the leader in the room who came up with the project says, "Oh no, I don't want to look at total customer base. I want to look at new customers. I want to look at acquisition, new customer acquisition. Let's look at that. Forget about customer base. That's a flawed measurement."

I've seen this happen many times. When the project sponsor doesn't see the results they want, they change how they're going to measure. This is why it's better to have those conversations up front about <u>how</u> to measure and talk this through. It is critical to get everybody's buy-in and document it so that you can remind people when you get pushback. "No, we said we were going to measure it this way. This was how we were going to measure it, and this was how we were going to know if we were successful."

b. Is the data available?

Secondly, data must be available and relevant. If you are expecting the team assigned to this project to measure results on a consistent basis, you will need to ensure that the data you are requesting is accessible in the frequency that you need it. Does your point-of-sale system only update new customer information once per day or once per week or at a different time schedule than the financial statements? Whatever you decide you need to count a new customer, make sure that your IT or data team is able to retrieve this information in the frequency and format that you need. Don't assume or take this for granted.

What about customer churn? If you decide to measure based on customer base numbers, how will you know that this partnership is the driver of the results you are seeing? Make sure that the data you have is segmented in such a way that you know if the results, good or bad, are truly due to new customers from this endeavor. Or could the results be because you're losing more or less of your existing base? Is your customer base growing because you're losing fewer customers, or is your customer base flat because you're bringing in lots of new customers with this new affiliate but losing all of them due to service failure or lack of inventory? If you're losing a lot of customers, you need to know that, even if you're gaining customers to replace them.

Even though the data needs to be accessible and relevant, remember what we talked about in the lesson on advancing change through courageous decisions. The data does not need to be 100% perfect in order to make business decisions. And it doesn't need to be perfect to drive results either.

 When you are developing reporting to drive results in your project, naturally you want the data to be as accurate as possible. But often, an obsessive focus on getting the measurement and reporting 100% accurate in order to understand if you are achieving the desired results is an avoidance tactic.

It could be conscious or maybe it's subconscious. Whatever it is, don't do it. You don't need your data to be 100% perfect. You are not preparing a tax return or a financial statement. You're not conducting an audit. You are developing a measurement to know if your project is successful. If you're off by a percent or two, it's not going to change the decisions that you'll make based on that information.

c. What are the mileposts we'll need along the way?

Finally, we need to set mileposts along the way. We've already learned that we need to define what our measurement looks like. We've talked about the data and making sure that we get at that data we need. We also need mileposts along our roadmap. If your goal is to grow customer base by 5% every year, where do you expect to be at the end of Month 1, Month 2 and Month 3? You get the idea. You don't want to wait a whole year to find out if you're going to achieve your results or if you're on track. And you don't want to load up the last quarter of the year, flounder for nine months and say, oh well, we'll get there, and then in December realize you're not even close to making your goal.

So you want to be sure to set mileposts along the way and figure out where you should be at the end of Month 1, Month 2 and Month 3 in order to make your annual goal. Be sure to take into account the seasonality of your business or any other factors that might determine the realistic nature of your mileposts.

To reach Syracuse on Day 11, we knew that we needed to be in San Antonio on Day 4, because we were spending three nights in New Orleans after that. So if you know that July is your slowest month, don't expect to gain the same number of customers as you do in September, which has historically been your busiest month. Consider those things when you set your mileposts. And again, as with everything we talk about, be realistic. One of the reasons we took a southern route was because we were making this trip at the end of March and knew that we could still have some winter weather in the north. It's important to consider weather, seasonality and the roadblocks you may encounter along the way. That's why mileposts are so important.

One of the reasons I think we miss the mark with this level of detail is that we get caught up in the excitement of the project and the idea of achieving results. This kind of detail doesn't feel so fun. It's not exciting. It's mundane. It feels nitpicky and overly detailed and controlling and often can be contentious within the leadership team, so we just gloss over it and don't do the hard work to ask these detailed questions. Plus, we've already done so much work to get this far. We've done all our work-around setting strategy and figuring out the right things to do and figuring out the projects that are going to drive that and frankly, we're a little weary. We just want to get the project started for God's sake. But trust me, it is crucial to ask these detailed questions.

All of these questions will come up at some point in the process, so if you're six or seven months in and the CEO is watching customer base remain flat and finally calls you one day and says, "Hey, I thought this affiliate marketing program was going to drive customer base. What's going on? I don't see it growing," you will be able to respond because you will know the answers to these five questions we've discussed. You will have thought it through.

Instead, so often what happens is that we wait until we receive that challenge from the CEO, or until we get that call about the project not delivering and then we scramble and try to reverse-engineer the answers. We gather the entire team in a conference room, wild-eyed and messy-haired, because it's becoming pretty clear we're not going to reach our goal, and the CEO wants to know whose fault it is.

You can avoid all that by addressing these questions ahead of time. Take your time to make the assignments. Take your time to figure out <u>what</u> you're going to do, <u>who's</u> going to do it, <u>when</u> you will be done, what your <u>why</u> is and the impact that you're hoping for, and <u>how</u> you will measure it.

As leaders, we can do a great job at the fun, sexy stuff like developing vision, setting strategy, figuring out what needs to be done and then leaving the details to our staff while we move on to something more worthy of our time and amazing leadership skills. We can sometimes view this level of detailed work as below our paygrade. **As a leader, it is your job to make sure this detailed work is done before the project is launched and that you have all the answers to the above questions.**

We have to plan our trip before we leave. We have to have the roadmap in place before we take off. Otherwise, we will waste time, money, resources, and worst of all, we will never get to where we wanted to go. We will not drive the results that we were hoping for. We will never get to the other coast. As leaders, we know we don't want that.

In the next chapter, we are going to continue our conversation about the ABCs of driving results, with a focus on the second element, B, and learn what we need to Beware of.

But first, let's have some time in the seat, because we know this is where the real magic happens. This is where we truly get a chance to practice our leadership.

Your Turn In The Seat

CASE STUDY

Think of a project that is happening right now in real time in your organization, even if it isn't a formal project. It doesn't matter if you're on the team or not. Perhaps you're hearing about it through your lunch buddy or your boss. Maybe it's hearsay or maybe you're leading the team.

1. <u>What</u> is the organization doing? What are they attempting to do?

2. <u>Who</u> is doing it? Who is on the team? Who's leading it? Who's the IT person? Who's the marketing person (or whatever the relevant departments are for this project)?

3. <u>When</u> is the deadline?

4. <u>Why</u> are you doing it? What is the impact that you're hoping for?

5. <u>How</u> is your organization measuring it? Have they defined that? Is it clear and manageable? Is the data accessible and relevant? What are the mileposts that have been set?

CHAPTER SEVENTEEN

BEWARE

The next key to success in driving results is for us leaders to BEWARE. Good drivers know that you need to keep your eyes on the road. We've all been told that from the time we were learning to drive. Why is that? Why is it so important to keep our eyes on the road? We know it's common sense so that we can see what's coming and be on the lookout for any flying mattresses. Remember the story about my niece driving down the highway at 65 miles per hour when a mattress flew off the car in front of her and hit her head on? We need to be looking out for those things or any other debris that might be in the road. We need to look out for danger and for weather. If it's going to hail or snow or there's an ice storm, or a tornado funnel off in the distance. We want and need to see those things ahead of time.

We also want to be able to read the signs that would alert us to a change in speed limit or a construction zone coming up, or a falling rock zone. It always makes me anxious to drive through a falling rock zone because I wonder what I would do if a big boulder fell in the roadway or on top of my car. We have warning signs for tsunami zones, landslide areas, steep grades, all those potential dangers that we need to beware of if we're going to be a good driver. There is an old railroad bridge in my hometown that hangs over a heavily traveled road, and every year a tractor trailer or a bus with a profile that is too high gets wedged under the bridge. Stuck and unable to move. The bridge has a clearance of 10 feet 9 inches and most tractor trailers are 13 to 14 feet. There are warning signs for miles leading up to this bridge telling drivers what the height clearance is. An elaborate warning system was even installed after a deadly crash a few years ago involving a double decker bus in the middle of the night. They crashed into this bridge and it shaved off the top half of the bus. It was horrifying. And yet, every year, professional and experienced truck drivers miss the signs. They're not aware of the danger lurking ahead and so they get themselves into a dangerous situation that could have been avoided.

As leaders, it doesn't matter how experienced or professional you've become or how amazing your leadership skills are. We must also be vigilant and keep our eyes on the road that our projects and initiatives are traveling down. We need to be cautious and guard against distractions and dangerous conditions. We need to know what's coming or if the project is stalling. We need to pay attention to these things because, as leaders, that is our job. That is what we're here for.

WE NEED TO BEWARE.

So what are some of the things that can prevent us from driving where we want to go? What are some of the things we need to beware of? In the context of projects in our organization, we need to keep our eyes on the road and look out for projects that are:

1. **Lost.**
2. **In need of a detour.**
3. **Stalled.**

1. Lost

When you're driving and find yourself lost, it simply means that you know where you want to go but you're not quite sure how to get there. Or maybe you thought you knew how to get there but took a wrong turn. Or maybe somebody gave you bad directions. Whatever the reason, you are wandering aimlessly or driving in circles.

As a leader, it's your job to check in on the project status. If you see a project team that seems to be going in the wrong direction, wandering aimlessly, driving in circles, you need to employ some strategies to get that group back together and headed in the right direction. One of the ways to do this is to review the decision-making process that you initially completed. Go back to your decision matrix that we learned about in Chapter 7. Review your quality decision that you made and remind everybody how and why you decided to undertake this project. That will help get everybody back on track, regroup, recenter and refocus them.

Also, you can revisit some of your Operational Excellence tools and strategies. Review the assignments that we covered in the last chapter. Review those details, every week if you have to, until you feel like the team is on solid footing. If you need to do it every week, especially in the beginning of the project, do it. **As the leader, you should be able to spot the signs and speak up if a wrong turn is being contemplated.**

I joined an organization once that had launched a project before I arrived, so I hadn't been there for any of the project scope development. I wasn't there for the decision matrix. I wasn't there for the pre-launch planning. The project was already in full swing. I could tell right away that it was floundering a bit. The project needed a leader, so I inserted myself into the process. I had a vested interest in the outcomes. We were replacing a dated system that required a lot of manual processes to support it because the technology was so limited.

It was apparent to me that the team had veered off-track. They were beyond project scope, they were spending a lot of time spinning in circles, and they had added a lot of unnecessary deliverables to the project. They were trying to do too much. As we've learned throughout this book, when you try to do too much, you don't get anything done. To be fair, the people who were trying to keep the project moving didn't have a lot of experience in this area and didn't quite know how to manage the programmers and the consultants, so they were lost.

It took some serious work, and a few radically candid conversations before we were able to get the team back on track. I met with the team and revisited what we were trying to accomplish and to clarify for them the destination that we were trying to reach.

Sometimes all it takes is to remind people of what the intention was, <u>what</u> we were trying to accomplish and <u>why</u>, and once again, to review all those assignments. It took months of repeating myself and reviewing the details about the project over and over again. More than a year later, we did get to where we wanted to go, but there was a period of time where the team was lost. The consultants and the programmers were lost too. They were so busy reacting to all of our demands that they were simply trying to keep up and give us what we wanted. We were all just circling, lost together. Getting the team back to the basics of our why, what we were trying to accomplish, was a key to this team finding their way again and then staying on track. **At times, the best thing you can do as a leader, is just keep everyone on the road.**

2. In need of a detour

The second thing that we need to beware of is when a project is in need of a detour. When something unexpected turns up in your lane, you may need to rethink your route. You may have a team that is doing very well operating on their own. They're clear about what they're trying to do, they're disciplined, they know how to stay on the road and they will stay on that road no matter what happens. They are determined, they've got their eyes fixed straight ahead, and they will follow the roadmap you've laid out for them. Unfortunately, this can be just as dangerous as the opposite circumstance, because unexpected things will happen that we need to beware of. Debris shows up in the road, a mattress flies in our face, the weather conditions change or perhaps the economic conditions change. Something changed after you made your plan, and now you need to reroute the team. You may still be going to the same place but you need to alter how you get there.

The COVID-19 pandemic was a great example of an unexpected circumstance that we did not see coming. I was working in the live events industry in California in March 2020 and as a result of the pandemic, we shut down the business for eighteen months. We would never have predicted something like this impacting our business the way it did. It was unexpected, a sudden shift in the road, a shift in weather that was devastating and threatened the survival and future of our business. We had to quickly find a detour, to pivot. We had to redirect a lot of projects. We had to stop some old ones and start some new ones. We had to guide the team through layoffs and furloughs, cash preservation and planning, all due to this unexpected hurdle in the road.

As a leader, you need to look out for those unexpected conditions, those things that block your road and guide your team to a detour in order to avoid disaster. It is your job to check in and keep your eyes on the road and make sure they are still on track to achieve what you all agreed upon.

3. Project stall

One of the most common enemies to any good project is project stall. We need to avoid project stall at all costs. When my husband and I first moved in together, he wanted to drive a few hours away to a Costco that was having a Kamado Joe roadshow. I had never heard of Kamado Joe and I had never heard of a roadshow at Costco. I asked clarifying questions. What are you talking about? What is a Kamado Joe? Roadshow? I learned that a Kamado Joe is a ceramic smoker oven. It's similar to the more well-known Big Green Egg, and they typically cost around $900. I thought my husband had lost his mind. This ended up being one of our first big negotiations as a couple. I had a hard time wrapping my head around the need to spend that much money on a grill. But after we had our discussion about the facts of this ceramic smoker—it is absolutely not a grill—I gave in. By the way, a roadshow at Costco simply means that you get a big discount on the retail price. I'll take that any day, so we jumped in the car and headed out of town. We brought the Kamado Joe home, my husband named her Ginger, and she's been on our deck ever since. We have realized a more than adequate return on investment, so I don't complain about it anymore. My husband was right.

We invited friends over for dinner one Sunday afternoon for pulled-pork sliders, which required Craig to smoke a pork butt in his new Kamado Joe. This is one of those cooking methods where you cook the meat low and slow for many hours. According to our calculations, we had plenty of time to get the meat to the internal temp of 200 degrees. We were humming along nicely, prepping side dishes and drinks. When our friends arrived, we hung out on the deck and had a few cocktails and watched the meat thermometer. It reached 160 and then it stopped moving. Craig started rummaging around the house for every different type of cooking thermometer we owned. We had electronic, Bluetooth, the old-fashioned dial kind, but they all said the same temperature. The meat was stuck at 160. It stayed there, and it stayed there, and it stayed there. We started to panic and after a few stress-filled hours of waiting for dinner, with our guests obviously getting hungry, we ordered pizza at 9 p.m.

Throughout this process, we did some Googling and research, and I learned something else that I hadn't heard of before, which was *meat stall*. It's a thing. Big pieces of meat that you cook low and slow can get to an internal temperature and just hang out there for hours. They stall. It's called meat stall. And you never know if it's going to happen. They don't always stall and you don't know when in the process it's going to happen or for how long they'll stay that way. Who knew? The next time we invited guests over for pulled pork, we cooked it a day ahead of time.

Projects and initiatives can stall just like our pork butt. You can be humming along nicely and then all of a sudden, you miss a meeting, miss a deadline, somebody's out sick or on vacation, or there are some distractions in the organization, and for whatever reason things just stop moving forward. You know you're in project stall when you have your weekly meeting and the update from the project team is the same report, week after week. Perhaps they're waiting for a phone call, or for the programmers to finish something, or they're waiting for the testing file. As a leader, you need to have your ears perked for this type of feedback occurring a few weeks in a row. Perhaps the person who usually gave the project updates stopped coming to the meetings. Maybe the project is not even on the agenda anymore, or you're sensing that the team is no longer excited or engaged in it. Be on the lookout for that. You probably won't have someone come to you and say, "Hey, boss, I think this project is stalled. You need to do something." **As the leader, it is your job to look out for the signs that the project is stalled.**

So, if you do encounter this in a project, what can you do? What can you do to avoid project stall? Or what can you do to get out of it if you find yourself with a temperature that isn't moving?

The first thing you can do is to make sure that you're providing the team with a way to prioritize and a way to wrap their arms around the project in a manageable way. Early in my career, I was working for a large public company with five or six business units. They were implementing a new general ledger and financial reporting package throughout the company and across all business units. It was a major project with a lot of stakeholders involved. As Assistant Controller for one of the divisions, I was assigned to the project team as the liaison for that division. This project had an eighteen- to twenty-four-month timeline to roll out. It was massive. The project lead who was tasked with managing this team taught me a valuable lesson that I've never forgotten. He held a weekly project meeting with representatives from all the departments and divisions. There were ten to twenty people in this weekly meeting, a group size that can be challenging to corral, but we had no choice. Every week, as we sat around the conference table, the leader passed around his agenda for the meeting, which consisted of what he had dubbed The Top Ten List. This list contained the priorities for the week. It was a very simple approach, but he was adamant about not going beyond ten items on that list. He got some pushback. The senior leaders, and even other team members, always wanted to add things to the list. Why can't we have twelve? Or fifteen? He held his ground and held the list to ten. As items were completed each week, we would add more, so it was a rolling top ten list, but we never went beyond ten for any week. I didn't realize this at the time, but now I know that **he knew that the bigger the list, the more overwhelming it would be for the team, and it would cause them to freeze or stall.**

Sometimes your teams will stall because they're trying to do too much. Also, he knew that in a one- or two-hour meeting, you'd never be able to speak in depth about the status of more than ten items. It's just too much to talk about in an hour-long weekly meeting. This lesson has stayed with me for more than twenty years.

Whether it is big projects or just meeting with my team one-on-one, I always try to limit the list of open items to five or even three, definitely not more than ten. Keeping the list small keeps the project manageable. The last couple of organizations I've been at, where we've held Operational Excellence team meetings, I would not let the list go beyond ten. Once your team sees that you're serious about it and gets into that rhythm, they appreciate it. They'll understand it and they'll stop trying to add to it. Then it becomes exciting to complete an open item and cross something off the list. **Your team needs wins.** That will also keep the project moving and prevent it from stalling. You've got to create that momentum.

Creating momentum to keep the team moving will help you avoid project stall. Your team needs wins, and managing and keeping your weekly priority list to a manageable amount is important. Don't fool yourself into thinking, "Well, my team can handle thirty items on their weekly list," "I need to push them or they're going to be lazy and not work hard enough," "I've got to give them stretch goals." Wrong. That doesn't work. It just overwhelms people and it overwhelms your resources. Everyone has a day job, there is only so much you can do. I don't care how important the project is, keep your list small and manageable. Give your team some wins. And for all those great ideas or priorities that come up but don't make the list because it's maxed out, write them down and put them in the parking lot, so that when a spot opens up, you can look at your parking lot and find your next priority to add to the list. This strategy helps for when your team, your leaders, or maybe even your CEO are pushing you to get a priority on the list, you can put it in the parking lot so they are assured you will not forget about it.

Creating momentum and keeping the team moving forward is critical. Make sure you're also taking the temperature of the team. Check in. Go to meetings. Even if you've been hands off throughout the project, start showing up. Make sure you go to a meeting or two a month, and if you don't have time, get updates from one of your direct reports. Again, if you see signs of project stall, you've got to step in. Otherwise, they will not get the result that you wanted. If you've been hands off, they may need a little push. You may need to do some old-school pop-the-clutch moves.

When I was a young teenager, we had this old VW bug that had more rust than paint and you could see the road through the holes in the floor. This car was a standard or stick shift, and I can't remember why, but there was a period of time when it wouldn't start. In order to start it, we would have to push the car and get it moving while the person in the driver's seat pushed the clutch in all the way to the floor. As I remember it, we'd put the car in second gear, somebody would push us down a little hill, and when we reached twenty miles per hour or so, we'd lift our foot and pop the clutch out and the car would start. It's very cool if you've never done it and exciting when you're a teenager.

As a leader, you may need to orchestrate an old-school pop the clutch. That's what we're here for. Remember, our leadership doesn't help anyone by staying in its office all day, or only going to senior leadership or executive meetings and not keeping our eyes on the road and on what's happening with our teams. We need to drive them. If we don't drive, something or someone else will.

Your Turn In The Seat

1. Have you ever witnessed a project that was **lost**? One that was way off-track from where they were headed? They took a left turn and just kept going the wrong way or maybe they went in circles for a time. Did they ever get back on the right road? What could have been done differently?

2. Have you experienced a project in need of a **detour**? Were there any projects in your organization in March 2020 that needed a reroute once the pandemic hit? Did you need to divert your team around some debris in the road? What was the detour that you came up with? Were you successful, or did the project crash and burn?

3. Think of a **project stall** that you've witnessed. How did you know they were in project stall? Did the team forget about this project or stop talking about it? Or did they keep coming to the meeting every week with the same updates, and it just got stalled for a while? How did it get moving again?

4. In your own personal leadership circle, how can you beware of all these things with your active projects? Are you using top ten lists? How are you prioritizing for your team? What are some of the dynamics you have going on that are unique to your organization, and what can you do to avoid a collision, or a crash and burn situation?

CHAPTER EIGHTEEN

COMMUNICATE

COMMUNICATION: WHAT IS IT? WHY DO WE NEED IT? HOW DO WE DO IT?

What is communication?

At its simplest form, communication is an exchange of information. It is delivering a message that is received in a timely manner by the intended party. **It is a message that you want to get to a specific audience in a way that they can digest and understand. It is information delivered in time so that it's relevant and useful in decision-making.** In the context of our work, we communicate expectations, deadlines and priorities for our team. We communicate coaching and feedback. We ask questions. We problem-solve. Communication is a two-way endeavor. We need to be listening as much as we are talking. There are studies that have shown that it's typical for people to spend between 70% to 80% of their day engaged in some form of communication, and that roughly 55% of our time is devoted to listening. We are not strangers to communication. It is something that we do a lot of all day, every day. As leaders, we deliver communication and are also on the receiving end.

Communication in the context of the ABCs of driving results is producing and delivering information about our projects and

initiatives, our priorities and strategic efforts, in order to achieve the outcome we need or to drive results.

There are many forms of communication. There is verbal, nonverbal, intentional and unintentional. There is the written word and the spoken word. We can use visual cues, audio and sensory communication. There's old-school email, hard copy reports, as well as the trendy and fashionable dashboards and Power BI tools. There are graphs, charts, narrative and PowerPoint presentations. I recently drafted a report for a Board meeting that was a combination of summary text (headlines), graphs and bullet points that I made in a PowerPoint deck. I printed to a PDF that was emailed out to the Directors. It was a summary of the financial results with headlines explaining the key takeaways I wanted them to have. Because there are some members of the board who respond well to narrative, there was also an eight-page report with updates from all the different departments within the organization. They received this information ahead of the virtual board meeting, during which I shared all of this on my screen and walked them through the materials. That was how I communicated the priorities for this particular organization. However, none of these details matter.

THE TOOLS OR METHODS WE USE ARE THE LEAST IMPORTANT ELEMENT OF COMMUNICATION.

Do not overthink or get too caught up in the vehicle you use to communicate. Use what is organic and currently available and relevant in your organization. If you can upgrade to a fancy new tool, great. If not, use what you have and what works for your audience.

At a previous company, we launched an exciting new BI tool called Domo. We were a very report-driven, report-heavy organization, with a lot of daily, weekly and monthly reports delivered mostly through email. These reports were generated from a few different systems, so creating this one landing page where we could all access our dashboards with our daily reporting was life-changing.

Whether you have a flashy, trendy dashboard, or send information out daily via email, don't get hung up on the communication tools. You can communicate whatever you need to, effectively and efficiently, regardless of the tools used. **Technology or lack of technology is no excuse for missing the mark on communicating to drive results.** Don't wait until you have the perfect tool or the fancy new gadget dashboard to communicate. If you have to write your message on a piece of paper and make copies of it and bring it to a meeting, then that's what you do. Or give your report orally. Whatever it is, don't let your communication tools, or lack thereof, stop you or be used as an excuse to not communicate like you need to in order to drive results.

WHAT IS MY MESSAGE?

What if I don't have anything new to say or report? What if I don't know what my message is?

The message that we need to deliver is directly tied to the first two elements of our ABCs of driving results. We need to communicate our assignments and then report on them consistently and accurately. We don't do all this work to keep it to ourselves. We know that in order to drive results, we need to answer these five questions: Who are you going to do? Who will do it? When will it be done? Why are you doing it (what is your why, or what is the impact that you're hoping for)? And finally, how will we measure it?

If you don't know what your message is or what you should be communicating in order to drive results, start with those five things related to your project or initiative and communicate those consistently.

Secondly, we also need to communicate anything that pops up on our radar screen or lands in our path, and all those things that we talked about in the last chapter on the subject of "Beware." If you have anything to report that has to do with a project not performing, not following the path that you thought it was going to follow, the team hitting a stall point, or something unexpected coming up and you need to figure out a detour, or if the project got off-track and is lost and you've had to rein in and refocus the team, you should be communicating all of that as well.

If you are struggling to figure out what your messaging should be or what you need to communicate about your project, start with the first two elements of driving results, ASSIGN and BEWARE.

Communicate on those topics consistently and accurately, and that will be a great starting point. Again, don't get hung up on the tools you're using to communicate or how you're going to convey your message and worry that it's not high-tech enough. Also, don't use the excuse that you have nothing new to report to avoid communicating about your project. You do have things to report. You can go through the five assignments that I just listed and give updates on those or just remind people about them. It can just be a five-minute update. Also, it can be, "Hey everybody, just a reminder, here's the assignments that have to do with this project. This is where we're at. This is how we're measuring it." That's it. Or a quick traffic report like this, "Boy, this COVID19 pandemic and the shutdown has really made it hard for us to execute on this project, so here's what we're going to do," or "We're looking into what we can do to keep moving forward in a new way." That's it. It doesn't have to be overly complicated. It's not rocket science. It's not brain surgery. You can do it. It can be very simple. **It's the <u>act of communicating</u> that is important, and that's what we're going to cover next.**

WHY DO WE NEED IT?

Why is communication so important? Communication is a powerful, dynamic, ever-changing, two-way force that is vital and necessary. It is the lifeblood of your organization. In fact, the life of your organization, your team and your success depends on communication. It is everything.

Communication sets the tone. Communication determines culture. Communication can motivate people. It can also tear people down. It can lift up, and it can destroy. It can be productive or destructive. It is powerful.

Most important, communication drives engagement. The word "engagement" has become another corporate buzzword in the last couple of years. Organizations have spent millions of dollars surveying their employees to measure employee engagement. Why? What does engagement even mean? What does engagement look like? What do engaged employees look like? They're passionate about what they do; they want to come to work every day; they are connected to the company's purpose; and they understand their role in the mission statement. They're committed and connected to their co-workers. That's what engaged employees look like.

Why do we suddenly care so much about employee engagement? When I started in my career, nobody was talking about employee engagement. Now everybody's talking about it because we've come to realize that if employees are engaged, this will drive a better performance from them, and employee turnover will decrease. We'll get better performance and better results, which translates to a better bottom line. That is why we measure employee engagement.

Engagement is also the cornerstone when discussing social media. If you sat in on a marketing meeting and played a drinking game in which you took a shot every time someone said the word "engagement," you'd be hammered at the end of an hour. In the world of social media, engagement refers to how many people are interacting with your post, your graphics, your topics, your content on Facebook, Instagram, Twitter, YouTube, wherever you are posting content. When social media first became a thing, especially a marketing tool, and we realized that there was real power to be harnessed, we thought it was all about the masses. We thought it was all about the big numbers, the quantity of followers we had, how many likes and how many "friends" we had. But, as we've become more informed and savvy in this realm and we have some track behind us to analyze, along with the infamous algorithms that determine how our social media is seen, we've come to realize that it's not just about the masses. It's not just about accumulating more followers, more likes and more friends. More followers doesn't necessarily translate to more customers or sales.

What we've come to realize is that the market today is saturated with social media content and activity, and that to stand out and to leverage social media in a way that is beneficial to our business, we need to engage with our audience. It's not enough anymore to just have an audience, we need to engage with them. We measure followers and likes and reshares and retweets. Why? Because we are convinced that it will ultimately drive sales of whatever we're selling. Social media engagement is a relatively inexpensive way to load up our sales funnel. And we know that, ultimately, the more social media engagement we have, the more sales we will close in that funnel. So, with both of these examples, with social media and with our employees, we measure and focus on engagement because, ultimately, we believe that if people are paying attention, they will remain committed to us.

 We want to cultivate this same dynamic in our organizations when it comes to our strategic initiatives and priorities. We need engagement. We need our staff to have passion, focus, commitment, and loyalty to our projects. This will keep them connected to the goal and will ultimately drive performance and results.

HOW DO WE DO IT?

How do we drive engagement? In social media, we do it through shares and retweets. We measure how many people have shared our post and retweeted our tweet. We want comments posted. Then, they're not just a follower, but they've read what we've posted, and they have something to say about it. Now we've entered into a two-way communication. We do still measure likes, even though they can be passive. When I'm passing through my Facebook feed, I can get into this zone where I'm automatically pressing like on my friends' posts. That doesn't necessarily mean I've read the whole thing or looked at all the pictures.

But we measure the stats, month to month and year over year. We measure the shares, the retweets, the comments, the likes, the followers, overall audience growth. We also measure click-through. How many click-throughs did we have from our social media content to our website? Why do we measure that? Our ultimate goal is to get them to our website so they can buy something. So that click-through measurement is very important when it comes to engagement. We also look for mentions. Has somebody mentioned our company or our brand out there on social media? If they have, we hope it's positive and will work for us and not against us. We use branded hashtags. All of these things drive engagement in the social media world. So that's what we measure.

How do we leverage communication in order to drive engagement when it comes to our projects?

In order to drive engagement and results with our projects, we need to be:

1. **Consistent.**
2. **Concise.**
3. **Relevant.**
4. **Authentic.**
5. **Relentless.**

1. Consistent. If we take our cues from social media, the first thing we need to do is to be consistent. Consistently post content. Have the update on your project every week or whatever the right frequency is for your organization. If you have a weekly staff meeting or a weekly management update, wherever you are reviewing the priorities of the organization and allocating resources, or trouble-shooting, or problem-solving, make sure that you consistently bring content to that meeting about your project. Let people know what's happening. If you have all-hands-on-deck meetings or an all-employee town hall once a quarter, and that's the only time you get in front of your group, then you need to have content at every one of those meetings about your initiative, so your staff sees it and they know it's something they need to engage with. They can't engage if you're not talking about it. If you're not posting any content to the team, they have nothing to engage with. So be consistent. People will learn to expect it from you. Consistently post content just like the experts tell us to do in social media.

2. Concise. We have short attention spans, and in today's culture and in our business world especially, our attention spans are shorter than they have ever been before. So make sure your content is easily digestible. Don't write a novel. I know it's hard to accept this, but no one cares about how long it took you to gather and analyze the data. No one cares about the cool macro you built to crunch the numbers or the complex pivot table with the V-lookups you use. They don't care. They just want to know how your results are tracking and if your expectations lined up with reality. They need to know if the organization is on track or not. Is it still a project? Do you still want me to engage with this? How's it going? **They need to know information quickly and they don't really care about the nitty gritty of the details. Keep it concise.**

3. Relevant. Know your audience. Understand what information they need and know what you need them to hear. Share content that people can understand and connect with. Share content that people can engage with. Keep it simple. But make sure it's relevant. When it comes to knowing your audience, don't prepare the same communication for your monthly directors meeting that you prepare for the quarterly town hall with all employees. Don't prepare the same report for your staff meetings and your department meetings that you prepare for the executive committee. Know your audience. Make sure your content is relevant to them. Make sure it's what they need to hear and what you need them to hear.

4. Authentic. The fourth element of how we communicate to drive engagement is to be authentic. In other words, are you being honest in your communication? Are you giving the good, the bad and the ugly? Are you telling people the real deal, no matter what? Bad news is tough to deliver, but there are ways to soften the blow. Sometimes we need to use grace and finesse to deliver bad results. I do not believe that open and honest communication means that you tell everyone everything all the time. There are things that we don't need to tell our teams or are unable to share yet with our staff. And there are certain things that we shouldn't communicate until we have all the information and facts. But often we use those situations to avoid communicating, and we need to check ourselves on that.

So what does it mean to be authentic and to have authentic communication? First, it means to be open. Be transparent and honest, receptive to feedback and questions. Build a culture where your team and staff feel comfortable talking to you if they are working on a project that is lost or stalled or in need of guidance. Make sure they feel safe coming to tell you whatever they need to tell you. And if they're not coming to you or talking to you, that's a red flag and a warning that you need to pay attention to. I recently sold some furniture on Facebook Marketplace, so I joined different garage sale groups on Facebook. Before they will approve you to be part of the group, you have to check a box and say that you agree to certain rules. Rules that typically ban political posts, religious posts, harassment and dark or offensive content. You must agree to abstain from any of that offensive behavior in order to join the group. Why? Because they want to keep a safe space where people feel comfortable engaging with your group. And if you have a bunch of people posting all kinds of polarizing and offensive content, people will avoid your group. They will disengage.

Build a culture in which people know you are open and receptive to feedback and questions. Be authentic. Be open. Be transparent. Be honest. Be someone who your team feels comfortable engaging with. In order to drive engagement, create a safe space through openness and honesty. Then, hold yourself and your team accountable. That's part of being authentic, too. You have to be honest. Don't sugarcoat the results. Whatever it is you're communicating about your project and the benchmark data that you're delivering, don't lie. Don't make it sound better than it really is.

We've all witnessed this throughout our career and maybe even participated in it for different reasons. We don't actually lie, or fudge the results, but sometimes we may not give all the information we have, especially if it's negative. We don't like to lead with headlines that tell employees that sales are actually trending down, or customer growth is going backwards. Sometimes we either leave out that benchmark because it's not trending the way it's supposed to, the project isn't being successful, or we look for a new way to measure until we find something that's trending positively.

I worked for an organization that had a bad habit of this and it was frustrating. Leadership would ask for analysis and reporting in a certain way, but if it didn't show the result they wanted, they would crumple the paper up, toss it in the corner of the conference room, and ask for a different analysis. They would keep asking and looking for that positive story that they could latch onto. Finding the positive story is important, of course. But honesty is more critical to your authenticity and engagement. You must keep yourself accountable. Don't sugarcoat results. We went through all that decision-making rigor earlier in this book. In the execute strategy and the advancing change modules, we talked about how to make a good quality decision. Even though you followed all of that guidance and disciplined approach, it is still possible to be wrong. It is still possible for a project to not work out the way that we were convinced it would. And that's okay. Remember, as an authentic leader, you are willing to be wrong, you are willing to make mistakes, to own them and move on. Leveraging communication to drive engagement is done through being authentic, honest, open, and by creating a safe space for people to engage with you.

5. Relentless. Finally, do not relent until the project is completed. Maintain focus. When you encounter stumbling blocks, figure out how to get around them, how to move them, and how to keep your project moving forward. Do not relent. When it comes to leveraging communication to drive engagement, we want to be consistent, we want to be concise, we want to be relevant, and we want to be authentic. If we do those things, we will drive engagement in our organizations. People will be engaged with our project. They will know that it is important to us. They will follow us. They will like us. They will remain tuned in. They will remain committed. They will know what's happening. And they will know that it's important to you if you do these things week after week, month after month, and do not relent.

Don't ghost your project. When somebody ghosts you, they stop answering your texts and stop engaging with you. There's never any formal breakup or ending of the relationship, they just stop engaging with you.

Don't ghost your projects. If you stop talking about a project or initiative, people will assume you've moved on. And if you go too long without talking about it, they will assume that the project is over, that nobody's working on it anymore. Remember, we only have so many resources in our organization. We only have so many people. We can only have so many priorities, and if we truly need this project to be completed, to be moved forward and to realize the results from it in order to execute strategy, advance change and drive results, then we must keep ourselves and our teams engaged.

If this project or initiative is one of your top three things to accomplish this year, but nobody is talking about it, people will forget about it. They will think you've ghosted it. We are all very busy. We need to keep our message front and center. If we don't consistently keep content in front of our audience, they will move on. We just will. That's how we're wired and how our society works right now. Don't ghost your projects.

Let's look at some guardrails or examples that use communication to hold ourselves and our teams accountable by measuring, tracking and publishing results in a way that is consistent, concise, relevant, authentic and relentless.

Guardrails

The following report is one that I used to communicate about the top three projects in our organization. Our No. 1 priority was to drive profitable growth. Now, that may sound like a no-brainer, but we really struggled to achieve growth with long-term profitability. We had no problem increasing top-line sales, but doing it in a way that also increased the bottom line took focus. I developed a one-page report to communicate updates and to keep people engaged with our initiatives.

I called it the "Roadmap to Profitable Growth." The page was split horizontally in three different sections. We attacked profitable growth with an initiative to drive revenue, one to manage and maintain margins, and then one to control expenses, because we knew we needed all three of those things to achieve profitable growth. My goal was to keep the team engaged with how we were defining profitable growth. The audience I was communicating with were from all departments and most did not have a finance background. So, below the table, I included a reminder of the definition of profitable growth so they had that context as they were evaluating the information. Profitable growth increases revenues, improves profitability, is sustainable over time, is primarily organic, and does not use unacceptable levels of capital. That was how we defined it in our organization.

Within each of the three sections: revenue, margins and expenses, I reminded them what our primary outcome was that we were working to achieve. What was our <u>why</u>? We wanted our sales to grow, we wanted our margin to improve by one point, and we wanted to reduce our expenses by millions of dollars. Then, I reminded them <u>how</u> we were going to do it. These are strategies that we said we were going to employ in order to make this happen. I included columns with the project owner name, a description of what we were doing, and the objectives or the measurable steps we were going to take. The information was specific. I included <u>what</u> we were going to do. The next column was <u>how</u> we were going to measure it. For example, first-time buyers year over year. Web sales dollars, co-op dollars, margin percentage. This was how we had all agreed to measure these initiatives. The next one to five columns had our estimated annual impact and what our benchmark was. We measured everything versus the previous year, so I included that number, as well as what our goal or budget was.

All of this information was consistently included in the report every time it was distributed. We set those at the beginning of the year. Here's what we said we were going to do, why we're doing it, who's owning it, and what we're going to measure. Every month, I updated the last three columns in which I reported our year-to-date results. I also gave a visual cue that was easy to zero in on if the CEO didn't have a lot of time. It was either a green arrow pointing up, a red arrow pointing down if we weren't on track, and if we were flat or right at our goal, I'd make a yellow horizontal line. The last column on the right had a space for notes, so if there was anything I needed to tell them about the project or any comments I needed to make, I had a place for it.

Everybody loved the format and raved about it the first time they received it. But often we develop these great one-pagers and initially everybody loves it, gets excited, high-fives you "great job," so we bring it to future meetings, but at some point, when it is not new and sexy anymore, we stop updating it. We forget to bring it. We ghost it. We just stop engaging with it.

This is when you need to be relentless. Update that damn report every month or every week, whatever the right frequency is for that project and for your organization, update it and bring it to every meeting you attend. In fact, have it out on your desk so that you always know where you stand with that project, and anybody who comes into your office can see it. They know it's important to you. They can engage with it. Then they will expect it. And six months in, if you don't bring it to the meeting, they'll ask you where that "Roadmap" is.

2022
ROADMAP TO PROFITABLE GROWTH

Goals	Strategies	Owner	Objectives	Measure (s)	Annual Impact	Benchmark	Goal	YTD Target	YTD Actual		Comments
Primary Outcome	How to Achieve		Measurable Steps			Last Year	2022 Target	3/31/2022	3/31/2022		
Sales increase 5% to prior year	Drive increase in sales to last year in all channels through improvements in customer experience	Susan	Increase first-time buyers through new return policy	First-time buyers vs prior year	$2M	$40M	$42M	$10.5M	$10.1M	→	Through March, team has struggled to gain traction
		Joe	Increase Member Web sales with free shipping/free returns	Web Sales	$3M	$60M	$63M	$15.75M	$15.75M		
Improve 1 margin point over last year	Reduce cost of goods sold through more efficient buying; take advantage of vendor discounts; improve pricing strategy on clearance items	Melanie	Lower purchase price 5%	COGS							
		Melanie	Vendor Discounts	Margin %						◆	
		Retail	Clearance Sales	Retail Margin						◆	
Reduce $5M	Reduce Marketing and Web Acquisition expense & manage all other to budgeted expense	Kate	Reduce Print	Print Expense	$1M	$5M	$4M	$1M	$1.5M	←	Promo Event in March
		Kate	Reduce Catalog	Catalog Expense	$2M	$7M	$5M	$1.25M	$2M	←	Catalog - decision to print catalog will impact original goal
		Jim/Mike	Reduce Web Acq	Web Acquisition	$.5M	$3M	$2.5M	$.625M	$.75M	←	Decision to spend more

PROFIT = $$$$

PROFITABLE GROWTH increases revenues, improves profitability, is sustainable over time, is primarily organic and does not use unacceptable levels of capital.

PROFITABLE GROWTH may be measured through sales growth, EBITDA, Net profit, Days of working capital and return on assets/investment.

Another example was developed at this company that struggled with short attention spans when it came to projects. We were high adrenaline, fast-moving, and things were changing all the time, so I needed something that was easily digestible. The financial planning and analysis group had a tendency to show all their work and all the numbers. They wanted everybody to see the five-page spreadsheet of columns and numbers, and at the very bottom of page five were the totals they needed to see to figure out what was happening. It was too much data and it wasn't effective. It wasn't driving engagement because it was too much for people to digest. It needed to be more concise. This one page was very visual. We had three major strategic initiatives. One was to drive sell-through at our retail partners, the second was to sell more units in a particular category, and the third was to drive our brand engagement. These three sections were outlined in three boxes, and the three key measurements for each were included.

I reported just the headlines. This is how our sell-through is trending with an up or down arrow with a percentage change to last year. I included the number of units and the average sale price. We had a couple of other key metrics around our club members. In the middle section, where we were trying to drive sales of more units, I included a simple graph with our annual goal. It was just a bar chart that let us know how we were trending and tracking as of the report publishing date. Finally, to report on driving brand engagement, we had statistics on followers, likes, reshares and tweets; who was talking about us, who was liking us, how many unique visitors this drove to our website. That was it. A simple one-page report, but for the particular audience I was communicating and engaging with, it was all I needed. Of course, we had all the details to back up the numbers, so if my boss or the CEO wanted to see them, we could share them.

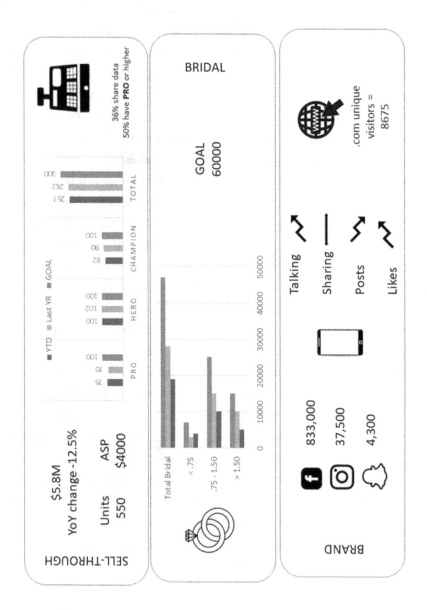

SELL-THROUGH

$5.8M
YoY change -12.5%

Units 550
ASP $4000

YTD Last YR GOAL

	PRO	HERO	CHAMPION	TOTAL
YTD	75	100	82	257
Last YR	70	102	90	262
GOAL	100	100	100	300

36% share data
50% have **PRO** or higher

BRIDAL

GOAL
60000

Total Bridal
<.75
.75 - 1.50
>1.50

BRAND

833,000
37,500
4,300

Talking
Sharing
Posts
Likes

.com unique
visitors =
8675

Take five!

Driving engagement through communication can be achieved by taking these steps and by making sure that you are effectively posting and promoting content that is resonating with people. Ultimately, this isn't about making people feel good. This isn't about people liking you or following you. This is about driving results, and if we don't have engagement, we will not drive results with our projects.

We must be engaging with our audiences about these projects or we will not get where we want to go. Remember, we are *Here to LEAD*, and our companies hire us to drive results.

Your Turn In The Seat

CASE STUDY

Whether it was an email report, or a fancy dashboard, or a PowerPoint presentation, find the last communication you produced about a project that is underway in your organization and review it. Answer these questions to find out if you are driving engagement with this project.

1. How often have you communicated about this project? Daily? Weekly? Monthly? If you can't find it or you don't remember the last time you communicated about it, that is a sign that you're not being <u>consistent</u> enough to drive engagement.

2. How long is the report? One page? Two? Is there too much information to easily digest? Is your report <u>concise</u>? Where can you make improvements?

3. Who is the audience for this report or information? Is the information that you're giving your audience <u>relevant</u>? Do you know what your audience needs to hear?

4. Are you communicating about this project <u>authentically</u>? Are you being open and honest with the facts? Do people feel comfortable giving you feedback, asking you questions, bringing you challenges or issues? Are you creating a safe space for engagement? If not, how can you change that?

CHAPTER NINETEEN

BONUS—REDUCE THE NOISE

INFLUENCING LEADERSHIP TEAMS: HOW TO REDUCE THE NOISE SO YOUR MESSAGE IS HEARD

Frances Hesselbein, former CEO of Girl Scouts of the USA and leadership guru, once said, "Communication is not saying something, communication is being heard." It is estimated that we spend approximately 70% to 80% of our day engaged in some form of communication and about 55% of our time listening.

The leadership teams we work for rely on our information, insight and influence to make the strategic business decisions that will drive the organization in the right direction. But if they can't hear our message, we're not successful.

We are subject matter experts based on our skills, experience and various departments that we manage. As such, we are the caretakers of the most important, most valuable, most critical items in the organization. We are the curators of the numbers. We provide to our leadership teams information, insight and influence.

It is our responsibility to communicate our expertise and what we know effectively and consistently, but more importantly, we need to be heard.

There is more "noise" in leadership teams today than ever before. We are inundated with data, numbers, analysis, news and social media. Our culture, including the business world, moves faster than ever. Leadership and decision-makers can often be so distracted by all this noise that they have a hard time hearing the messages they need to hear. They miss the real KPIs and trends because they are so distracted.

We need to look for creative ways to get the attention of the leadership team, get them focused on what's important, make sure they see and hear the real story. This applies to all communication, including daily, weekly, monthly reporting, as well as budgeting and ad-hoc analysis.

One Saturday morning, I was driving my stepson to his volunteer job at the San Diego Humane Society. I needed to drop him off at 7:30 a.m. so he could be on time and so I could make my 8 a.m. boot camp class in Mission Bay. I had been to this place once or twice, so I was fairly sure where I needed to go, but I wasn't 100% confident. As we were getting closer, I began to doubt myself. I wasn't sure where to get off the freeway. I said to Garrett, "Hey, can you Google Map the address? I need to know which exit to get off."

He didn't verbally respond but I saw him playing with his phone out of the corner of my eye, so I thought he was doing what I had asked. I had my eyes on the road, paying attention to the cars around me. The exit was fast approaching and I still hadn't heard from him.

"Is this the right exit?" I said, "What does your phone say? Should I get off here?"

I was anxious because of his silence and let the exit pass by and stayed on the freeway.

I spoke a little louder and waved my hand at him. "Garrett, was that the exit? Did you get it on your phone?"

Out of the corner of my eye, I saw him remove an ear bud before he looked at me and said, "Huh? Did you say something?"

"Garrett! Yes, I was talking to you. You didn't hear me?"

"No, sorry, I was listening to music."

He hadn't heard a word I'd said because he had other noise in his ear interfering with my voice. Needless to say, we missed the exit and had to drive an extra ten minutes out of our way to get there. Both of us eventually arrived where we needed to be, but we were late.

If your audience doesn't hear the important things you have to say at the appropriate time, the organization and the leadership team could get off-track, perhaps get lost for a while or take a wrong turn. They may eventually get to the right place, but it could take them longer than it should.

I've worked in a variety of companies—big, small, corporate, entrepreneurial—with different cultures, expectations and resources. But the one consistent thing I've seen is that oftentimes it can be difficult to get your audience to hear what you need to tell them.

NOISE

Noise is defined as any sound that is undesired or interferes with one's hearing of something; loud, confused or senseless shouting or outcry; irrelevant or meaningless data or output occurring along with desired information.

We all have our pet peeves when it comes to noises that bother us. Here is my short list: the sound of my husband, or dog, crunching on something in the living room; the rumble of snoring while I'm trying to fall asleep; extra loud video games or action movies with gunshots and car chases as the only form of dialogue.

At work, the list of noises that interfere with my peace and quiet are too many people in a meeting; overwhelming information dumps; analysis paralysis or non-financial people distributing numbers that don't tie to the financial statements. What noise do you have in your organization? Have you ever had someone outside your department produce a report with information about your results and bring it to a meeting without first reviewing it with you, especially if you're a finance person and you're responsible for all the numbers? Maybe somebody in shipping produces an Excel spreadsheet with numbers that don't tie to the financials. You haven't laid eyes on them yet so you have no idea if they're accurate, or if the timing was right, or if it agrees with your messaging and what you've been reporting to the leadership team.

We're all human beings with these egos, and everybody wants to be heard. Have you ever been in an organization where the culture is such that everyone is vying to get a sentence out, even if it's not relevant, or meaningful, or correct? They just want to talk so they can be noticed at the meeting. Individual agendas and people having their own priorities at the cost of whatever else is going on around them also create noise in an organization.

WHO OR WHAT IS MAKING ALL THIS NOISE?
Noise in an organization can be both external and internal.

External noise comes from:
- **Industry.**
- **Culture and perception.**
- **Data and technology.**
- **Politics and news.**
- **Experts and analysts.**

Industry
What's happening in your industry right now? What are the headlines? Is there consolidation happening? Or the opposite? Are new startups threatening the landscape? When I was in the athletic footwear industry and the jewelry industry, we had the competing dynamics of the traditional "mom-and-pop" retailers and the national chains. I worked in the live events industry during the COVID-19 pandemic. Our venues were shut down for more than eighteen months with uncertainty as to when and how business would return to normal. There was so much noise that it took a significant amount of focus and patience to wade through it and find what the facts truly were.

Culture and perception
What is the current state of your organization's culture and the perception of your customers and employees? Whether you're in a customer service call

center, or managing a subscription/membership service, when that group receives five calls with upset customers or cancellations, suddenly there is a huge problem. The building is on fire and the company is headed toward disaster. Somebody sends an email, the CEO panics, and before you know it, a meeting is scheduled to develop a plan of attack. We may have 749,990 happy customers, but because those ten called today, we think we have a problem that needs our immediate attention. This is just noise that could potentially distract you from more important or pressing issues.

There is also the culture of our world and society around us that is a major force, and even if it doesn't directly impact your business or industry, it is affecting your employees who live in this world. The pandemic, racial injustice, social unrest, mass shootings, stimulus packages, all of these create noise.

Data and technology

We are very dependent on our systems, yet they can cause a lot of disruption, even when working as planned. Organizations have cobbled together legacy systems with new technology, and typically spend as little as they can get away with. Often, we let the systems determine our process instead of the other way around. Also, if good controls are lacking, and error reports are not in place, or no one is monitoring them, issues such as orphaned transactions, incomplete orders or duplicate credit card charges can accumulate.

Politics and news

We survive presidential elections every few years. Election activity can disrupt markets, cause conservative decision-making and disrupt consumer behavior, at least temporarily. A headline on Yahoo or CNN, whether it is real or fake news, or a video gone viral, can shake up a business within seconds.

Experts and analysts

Then there are those professionals who may have information about your industry, about your company or your customers. Maybe it's the latest marketing trends or latest retail trends. Whatever it is, it can create noise in your organization. What's happening in your industry right now? What are the headlines? Is there a consolidation happening or the opposite, or new startups threatening the landscape? During the pandemic in the live events industry, there was a lot of uncertainty. Experts were scrambling to figure out what to do, and how we were going to come back from this pandemic, and what our industry would look like after this worldwide health crisis. Would we come back? Would patrons ever want to attend a live show again, and what would that look like? Surveys were distributed and published on a weekly basis. New technology emerged. So much noise. It took a lot of discipline to not react and not overreact and let things settle a bit and sift out what was true information and insight, and what was just noise.

As leaders, it is our job to learn which noise is distracting and which noise we actually need to pay attention to. It is also our job as leaders to make sure that we are heard in spite of the noise. Along with external sources, noise can be generated internally.

INTERNAL NOISE COMES FROM:
- **Others: perceptions, perspective and power struggles.**
- **Me: It's us...look in the mirror.**

Others: Perceptions, perspective and power struggles
All departments in an organization are competing for resources and leverage. Bad behaviors, departmental silos, resistance to change and lack of accountability can all influence our perceptions and perspectives. Power struggles are real. Stereotypes and profiling are rampant in the organizations we lead. Here are some preconceived perceptions I've witnessed:

The sales team doesn't pay attention to detail. They'll do anything or say anything to get the sale. They only care about the top line and their commission. You can't trust them.

Marketing just wants to spend money, but they are clueless when it comes to operations and the customer. They have no idea what it's like to actually wait on the customer at the register and try to accommodate the promises they've made in their advertisements.

Merchandising just wants to buy inventory and load up our backrooms and sales floors. They don't pay attention to turn or obsolescence.

IT is in their own world and you can't talk to them. They don't care.

Operations just wants to bulldoze and boss everyone around.

Finance is full of bean counters who just like to say no because they can.

Retail believes they are the only ones who make any money for the company and wholesale thinks we owe our entire existence to them.

Corporate admin departments like facilities, human resources and accounting never get noticed unless they screw up and are sometimes treated like they bring no value because they are perceived as not directly impacting the bottom line.

Sound familiar? All of these belief systems are at play and contribute to noise.

You must understand the perceptions, perspectives and power struggles in your organization so you can communicate *in spite of them.*

Me: It's us…we need to look in the mirror

The harsh reality is that a lot of the time we have no one to blame but ourselves. It's my fault. It's us. It's you and me. The reason our message isn't being heard is our fault and no one else. We mumble and are sloppy. We're not confident or loud enough, so we ramble or we whisper.

I was in a meeting once and the only incorrect item on my entire report was the date in the upper left-hand corner of the spreadsheet, but the audience questioned the entire thing. I made one small error on a report that I handed out, and suddenly everybody in the room stopped listening to me. They tossed the page aside and moved on to the next item on the agenda. I was left sitting there with my mouth open. I wanted to say, "Wait a minute, it's just the date. Everything else is correct." But I had lost them. It was too late. I lost their confidence. This happens when we're sloppy.

HOW CAN WE BE HEARD?

N.O.I.S.E.
- **N**eed to know.
- **O**wn your message.
- **I**...look in the mirror.
- **S**peak their language.
- **E**liminate noise when you can.

<u>N</u>OISE
Need to know

1. Make sure YOU know what your message is—what are you trying to say?
2. Make sure you know what THEY need or want to hear—what do they need to hear?
3. Don't be afraid to lead with the HEADLINES.

Whether you are creating a recurring report, or a simple email, be sure to take a moment to step back and carefully review what you are about to send or distribute. Does it say what you want it to say? Is it clear? Does it respond to what your audience asked you for?

Lead with the headline. Grab their attention, whether it is in written form on the page, or you are presenting at a meeting. Give them the most important takeaway first before they begin to filter what you're saying. When we have worked long and hard on a project or analysis, we are invested. And we think everybody wants to hear about our methodology and process and the assumptions we made. Especially if you are in finance. I can relate because I'm one of you. We like to go through every detail. We like to show our work. We want to go through all the brilliant analysis that we did, because it was such hard work. All this number crunching took us hours and hours and hours. We have a beautiful spreadsheet, plus we want them to believe us. We want to start at the bottom and show all our work and tell them how we got there. But sometimes, this is just noise, and we could lose the audience in the first thirty seconds of speaking.

Lead with the most important takeaways. Lead with what you want them to walk out of that meeting with. Once you do that, you can circle back around and go through your detailed work. You can answer questions. Somebody in the room is sure to ask how you arrived at your conclusion.

Even though our ears are capable of picking up many words, our brain doesn't necessarily process all of them. Most people usually only remember about 17% to 25% of what they hear. This means if you have fifteen minutes on the agenda, your audience will only absorb and remember three minutes of what you say. Give them the most important takeaway first before they begin to filter what you're saying.

I had a colleague once who used to tell his team, "Don't tell me about the current and the conditions and the size of the waves or the near disasters— tell me when the ship is in port."

NOISE
Own your message
1. **Be clear.**
2. **Be confident.**
3. **Repeat.**

This is easier said than done. How many times have you been in a meeting, handed out your spreadsheet, and as everyone is passing it around, noticed a number that is wrong? It's staring you in the face. Your stomach drops. You start to sweat. You stammer. You can't take the pressure, so you confess your sin to the room, and then you lose them. The spreadsheet goes to the bottom of the pile and your time on the agenda is wasted. What we don't realize is that chances are, your audience won't notice the mistake. So what should you do if this happens? Fake it. If the number in error doesn't change the outcome or the message, do not mention it. Fix it when you get back to your office and send out a corrected version if you need to. If it's not a material error, it doesn't change the outcome, it doesn't change your headline or the takeaway, so just plow through it confidently and clearly. Repeat.

However, if the error is blatant and it changes the outcome or your message, of course, be up front about it. Be an authentic leader who is willing to be that vulnerable. Pull the report back and promise follow up. End of story.

This happened to me recently. I was presenting summary information about the fiscal year budget to department heads who were non-financial people. As I was talking, I began to question a few numbers on my slide. They seemed off but I wasn't sure if they were wrong or not. For this particular audience, it didn't matter. The message I wanted them to hear was in regards to other non-financial KPIs and I needed them to stay focused. So I didn't mention it and finished my presentation. Immediately after the meeting was over, I checked my numbers, and they were right, but needed a footnote explanation for future reference. I had done the right thing by not interrupting the conversation or losing confidence. That would have created noise during this presentation.

Never let them see you sweat. If you lose confidence in your message, so will your audience.

NOISE
I need to look in the mirror
1. FRAME your work.
2. Your TEAM reflects you.
3. Listen.

The only thing we ever have control over is ourselves and hopefully our department or direct reports. I was leading a financial reporting and analysis team that was hardworking, intelligent, creative and knew their way around a complex Excel file or database. They could run circles around me when it came to the technical part of the job. However, with my background and early years spent in public accounting, I had a much more disciplined approach to the output we were creating. Our team had developed some bad habits of completing and distributing reports with errors, poor presentation and formatting, incorrect dates, inconsistencies with headers, footers, titles, etc. They were a smart and talented team, but they were more concerned with finishing their reports quickly and were not taking the extra few minutes to properly format and check for accuracy. I tried addressing this through lecture and serious discussion, but I just didn't seem to be having an impact. This team provided most of the reporting in the organization and because of these issues, they were creating the noise that prevented their own messages from being heard and it had impeded their reputation and trust with others.

I wanted to find a way to address the team using an informal, lighthearted/non-threatening approach because I didn't want to de-motivate them. I asked them to help develop an acronym (if you haven't noticed yet, I do love an acronym) that would provide us all with a uniform approach to making sure any and all reports distributed from our department met certain standards.

We began to use **F.R.A.M.E.D**. as our acronym. This gave us a talking point and perspective that we could use in our daily conversation. For example, instead of questioning someone's accuracy, I could say, "Hey, is that report FRAMED correctly?" or "Good job on getting the report done, but it doesn't look like it was FRAMED properly. Take another look at it." Also, the team members could hold each other accountable and ask their teammates, "Can you take a look at my work and make sure it's FRAMED correctly?"

I had Scrabble trays made with the acronym in letter tiles for each team member and they kept them on their desk.

FORMAT: Does it print properly? Is it readable in all applications—email, mobile, desktop? Does it have proper titles, column headers, page header and footer? One of my biggest pet peeves is when I get an Excel file, or a Word document, or anything, and it's not formatted for printing in case I want to print it. That drives me crazy. Format.

READABLE: Is the font a reasonable size? Is there enough white space on the page? Is it easy to read? If you make your font small because you want to fit it all on one page, is anybody going to be able to read it at the meeting? Remember, not everybody has 20/20 eyesight. You have to consider that. Is it readable?

ACCURATE: Does the column "foot", which means if you take a calculator and add up the column of numbers, does it equal the subtotal on the report? Have you tested it? Have you double-checked it? Are columns summing properly? Are the variance formulas correct? Are there formula errors that are showing up?

MAKE SENSE: Does the report make sense to you and to the audience? Does it make sense as compared to last week's report? Is it consistent to what's been happening in the business? If, for the last three months, your sales have been on a consistent upward trend and have been up 2% every week over last year, and now you're working on this week's report and sales have plummeted by 35%, double-check it. Make sure it's right.

ELIMINATE CLUTTER: Has all unnecessary information been eliminated from the page? If it doesn't need to be there, get rid of it. Remember, we want it to be easy to read. We want to make sure our message is heard. Clutter on a report is just noise. It's going to distract people from what you're trying to get them to pay attention to.

DATES: Is the date of the report correct? Are you reporting the correct timeframe—month, year or other period? If you're doing February's report, make sure it doesn't still say January, and you've updated the date in the upper left corner. Have you met the due date? Is the date of the report included in the footer?

NOI$E

Speak their language
1. **Be creative in delivering messages.**
2. **Change your frequency.**
3. **Realize not everyone has your same perspective or experience.**

Be creative in delivering your messages. Change your frequency. Realize that not everyone has your same perspective or experience. For example, if your background is finance and accounting, consider that not everybody had five years in public accounting. Not everybody has an audit or a tax background. Not everybody understands debits and credits. That's why they need accountants. Be sure you're not using a condescending tone to others who are outside your discipline or area of expertise.

I delivered financial updates on a quarterly basis to an extended staff, which included the CEO, VPs, directors and department heads. It was a diverse audience with varying levels of financial acumen. I was having mixed results with my messaging. I was frustrated. I felt like people weren't really understanding where we were headed. I wanted to make it a little fun and memorable, so I looked for creative ways to get my point across.

I brought a plate of chocolate chip cookies and passed them around the room as I started my presentation. I began with a slide that had a Betty Crocker recipe for chocolate chip cookies. It was a traditional recipe that talked about the flour and the butter and the sugar and the chocolate chips and the egg. Everybody had a laugh, and everybody was eating cookies.

My next slide was a recipe for profit. My list of ingredients was $500 million of revenue, $200 million in gross margins, $10 million in other revenue, $5 million in co-op expense, 5% to ship our orders, 8% marketing expense, 20% in employee expense. All of these different elements got us to the profit number that we were trying to create.

The message I wanted to convey to the team was that if we were missing one of the elements of the recipe, we need to make an adjustment to the other line items. If we don't have a cup of flour, we need to reduce the sugar. If I'm going to make a recipe and cut the flour in half, I need to cut the sugar in half. If we aren't achieving our $500 million in revenue, we can't spend the planned dollar amount in other areas. We need to adjust the spending to the level of revenue. Otherwise, we won't achieve our desired result.

This example was lighthearted in nature, but that's okay. It actually worked very well and drove the message home. Not only that, people remembered it. I could refer back to it and say, "Do you remember our recipe for chocolate chip cookies? If we don't have all the flour, we can't use all the sugar. So if we're not getting all our revenue, we can't spend all our money." We don't have to be serious all the time.

Ingredients

- **2 ¼** cups Gold Medal™ all-purpose flour
- **1** cup butter or margarine, softened
- **¾** cup granulated sugar
- **¾** cup packed brown sugar
- **1** teaspoon vanilla
- **1** egg
- **1** teaspoon baking soda
- **½** teaspoon salt
- **1** cup coarsely chopped nuts
- **1** package (12 ounces) semisweet chocolate chips (2 cups)

Ingredients

- **$500M** Revenue
- **$200M** in Gross Margin $
- **$10M** in other revenue
- **$5M** in Co-op
- **5%** to ship our orders
- **8%** Marketing
- **20%** in Employee expense
- **8%** Occupancy
- **9%** Other

PROFIT!

At another meeting, I was trying to convey to the leadership team that even if they weren't in the finance department, they still needed to know certain key numbers for the organization. I did a play on the American Heart Association's "Know Your Numbers" campaign. The American Heart Association annual campaign challenges us to know our cholesterol, blood pressure, blood sugar and our BMI. As we discussed my slide, I asked the group, "In our organization, what are those four numbers that we all need to know?" It was our revenue, our margin, our expenses and our profit. I began reporting out those four numbers at every meeting and challenged the team to remember them.

cholesterol*blood pressure*blood sugar* bmi

1	Revenue	1	_____
2	Margin	2	_____
3	Expenses	3	_____
4	Profit	4	_____

At a budget kick-off meeting, I talked about New Year's resolutions and translated the nature of a New Year's resolution to a budget goal—they need to be realistic and possible, require effort and sacrifice, and push us to be better.

These examples and guardrails reflect the organizations and leadership teams that I was in at the time. Yours may look different. Sometimes we're in our own little world, in our own little bubble. We think everybody should just understand what's coming out of our mouths. That's just not always going to happen. Know what that is for you and your organization. The team I was on at the time did have a sense of humor. They could be fun and playful. If you're in a super serious organization, you may want to try something different. But consider your audience and the language they speak, and see if you can present your message in a creative way.

NOISE

Eliminate noise when you can
1. **Look for opportunities to eliminate distractions.**
2. **Give up the need to be right.**

You're a leader. Eliminate noise when you can. Look for opportunities to eliminate distractions and give up the need to be right.

When I first joined the senior team at one organization, there were distractions that I noticed right away. As the senior finance leader, others made sure to tell me about a few problems and "inaccuracies" with the reports coming from my department. Of course, my first instinct was to put my guard up and be defensive. But instead, I listened and asked questions. I reviewed the facts with my team. The truth was, we (the finance team) were right. The audience that we met with weekly to discuss company results and roundtable and brainstorm business initiatives was getting hung up on the wrong things. Week after week, we tried to teach, to explain, to provide more information, to get them to look at the right headlines and takeaways, but we just could not overcome this hurdle with them. There was only one thing left to do. We had to give up our self-righteous need to be right. Sometimes we can stubbornly refuse to change our message, and instead dig our heels in until our audience gets it. But if you try this and it doesn't work, you are allowing noise to drown out your message. Eliminate the issue.

Another example at the same organization was noise caused by the way we were recording deferred revenue on a monthly basis. It was causing major shifts on a P&L line item. Although it was just an accounting entry to adjust a balance sheet account, and it was a non-cash item that was not driven by operations, this fluctuating number drove my CEO bonkers. If it was a month with a big shift, or it varied significantly from last year or budget, we could not move on to the important items in my update. So I worked with my team to eliminate this monthly adjustment. The reality was that on an annual basis we didn't see much change, it was the seasonality throughout the fiscal year that caused the disruption. Our auditors only cared about the year-end number, and it didn't impact our bank covenants. So we stopped recording the monthly journal entry. It was as easy as that. We continued to evaluate our balance sheet account, and if we saw a trend that might change the annual number we were expecting, we were prepared to deal with it. But this small change made a huge difference in my monthly meetings with the CEO when we reviewed financials. I could finally get him to hear what I needed him to hear.

Making sure our message is heard is one of the most important things we can do to ensure our organization is generating the right decision and heading in the right direction.

Your Turn In The Seat

1. What are your pet peeves when it comes to noise? At home and at work?

2. What are the external noises? Think about each one of these and write down relevant observations.
    a. Industry.
    b. Culture and perception.
    c. Data and technology.
    d. Politics and news.
    e. Experts and analysis.

3. What are the internal noises in your organization? Think about each one of these and write down relevant observations.

    a. Others: Perceptions, perspective and power struggles.
    b. Me: It's us...we need to look in the mirror.

4. Are there any messages that you are trying to communicate that have not been heard because of noise? What is causing the noise? More importantly, what can you do to reduce the noise so your message is heard? Review the elements of N.O.I.S.E. to find an opportunity to make changes.

Headlines

✓ The ABCs of **DRIVING RESULTS** are:
   a.   Assign.
   b.   Beware.
   c.   Communicate.

✓ **Assign:** There are five assignments that we need to clearly make when launching a project or initiative that is going to execute strategy and/or advance change. Here are the five:
   a.   <u>What</u> are you going to do?
   b.   <u>Who</u> will do it?
   c.   <u>When</u> will we be done?
   d.   <u>Why?</u> What is your why or the impact that you're hoping for?
   e.   <u>How</u> will we measure it?

✓ **Beware:** We need to keep our eyes on the road and look out for projects that are:
   a.   Lost.
   b.   In need of a detour.
   c.   Stalled.

✓ **Communicate:** In order to drive engagement and results with our projects, we need to be:
   a.   Consistent.
   b.   Concise.

    c.   Relevant.

    d.   Authentic.

    e.   Relentless.

✓ **Influence:** Reduce the N.O.I.S.E. so your message is heard:

    a.   <u>N</u>eed to know.

    b.   <u>O</u>wn your message.

    c.   <u>I</u>...look in the mirror.

    d.   <u>S</u>peak their language.

    e.   <u>E</u>liminate noise when you can.

CHAPTER TWENTY

THERE IS NO LEADERSHIP HACK

Congratulations! You have made it through the four anchors of leadership. You've done the work. The four anchors are:

1. **Leadership.**
2. **Execute Strategy.**
3. **Advance Change.**
4. **Drive Results.**

These four anchors will help us become the authentic leader that we so desire in our heart of hearts. These anchors will keep us steady when the waters are rough and tethered when we tend to drift. Rather than wandering aimlessly or being tossed about by every trend, every challenge, or the highs and the lows of our career, these anchors will provide the footing we need to be consistent, reliable and effective, day after day. After all, that's what we're here for.

We are *Here to LEAD*. I cannot stress this enough, and I know I've been repeating myself throughout this book, but I'll say it again anyway. Our organizations hire us because they need leaders. Why do they need leaders? They need leaders to get stuff done. They need leaders to help execute strategy. They need leaders to advance change throughout the organization. And they need leaders to drive results. That is what our leadership is for. If you've been paying attention for the last nineteen chapters, this should be old news.

We began this journey by studying leadership. We learned that in order to be a leader, we must aspire to it, we must study, and most importantly, we must practice being a leader. Then, we talked about developing our own elevator pitch of leadership and intentionally putting down on paper and internalizing what leadership means to us.

In Section Two, we learned the common reasons why we aren't successful in executing strategy:

1. **Try to do too much.**
2. **Let the day-to-day priorities steal our time.**
3. **Do the wrong things.**

Then we covered <u>how</u> to Execute Strategy and the things we need to do in order to accomplish this. To Execute Strategy, we must:

1. **Resist the urge to do too much.**
2. **Protect our time.**
3. **Do the right things.**

We know how to determine those projects and initiatives that will drive us toward strategy execution. We now know that limiting ourselves in the number of projects that we try to accomplish, resisting the urge to do too much and making the time to Execute Strategy is critical. We discovered useful and powerful guardrails in that section like the Red Light Green Light decision matrix and the Crossroads graph. These two tools will help you make quality decisions in your organization.

In Section Three, we learned about advancing change. Change is hard and it is human nature to resist it due to:

1. **Physics.**
2. **The loss we associate with it.**
3. **The determination required.**

We learned that advancing change can be accomplished despite these obstacles with:

1. **Operational excellence.**
2. **Courageous decisions.**
3. **Time.**

CHANGE IS THE INTERSECTION OF DISCERNMENT, DISCOVERY AND DETERMINATION.

Finally, in the last section, we mastered the ABCs of driving results. Which were:

Assign

Beware

Communicate

The bonus chapter on influencing leadership teams by reducing noise in your organization so that your message is heard is a valuable guardrail that is critical for all of us.

The purpose of *Here to LEAD* is to provide you with practical tools that you can tailor to whatever is going on in your life, in your career, or in your organization at any time. It is very important that you take the time in the seat and do the exercises at the end of each chapter. Go through the guardrails and examples in this book and think about how you can relate these to your world. These tools, these guardrails, these lessons, are the anchors of your leadership. Remember, anchors hold us in place, they keep us from drifting, and keep us tethered to what's important.

Leadership is important to us, to you, to me. That's why we're here, that's why you're reading this book—because effective leadership is important to you.

One of the pitfalls that leaders like you and me often fall into is that we think there is some silver bullet or magic pill out there that will instantly transform us into the leader we need to be in all seasons of our life and career. There isn't. Also, you will be tempted to overcomplicate your leadership. Resist that temptation.

You will be tempted to keep searching for some leadership hack. Don't. It doesn't exist.

THERE IS NO LEADERSHIP HACK

Life hacks are all the rage right now. A life hack is a shortcut, a trick, a newfound skill to do something faster, easier, more creatively than we have before, usually in the interest of saving time, money or work for ourselves. I'm sure you've seen them online, in social media, or perhaps on YouTube, TikTok, Facebook, and Instagram. There are hacks all over the place to do all kinds of things. Maybe you've learned of some the old-fashioned way, by word of mouth.

The term "life hack" is a fairly new term that we use to refer to shortcuts, but the concept itself, the idea, isn't new. Back in the Eighties, we had hacks like spraying hydrogen peroxide on our hair and smearing baby oil all over our skin and laying out in the sun. That was a hack, a shortcut, to try to get the sun-drenched beach look without actually putting in the time at the beach.

I had a piano while growing up and took traditional piano lessons and learned the old-fashioned way how to play. I studied the basic concepts of how to read music, practiced the scales, and learned all the foundational concepts. A few years ago, I got another piano and started playing around on it again, trying to remember all those things I had learned as a kid. I discovered there are many piano "experts" trying to come up with the hack that will teach anyone the piano without having to put in all the time that we used to think we had to put in. There are so many YouTube videos on how to learn the piano faster, easier, how to learn chords, and promises like, "If you learn these four chords, you can play any song." I have fallen for a lot of those advertisements and tried quite a few of them.

I've seen hacks on how to squeeze avocado meat out of the fruit if you don't have a knife. How to open a wine bottle without a corkscrew. Remember when that hack was viral a few years ago? You put the wine bottle in a shoe, then banged the shoe up against a wall, and the cork fell out.

I do love a good hack. My personal favorites these days usually involve cooking. I've watched my husband try so many different hacks for peeling garlic—shaking it in Tupperware until the skin comes off, or heating in the microwave for ten seconds or so, and then the cloves pop right out of the bulb. Then there's a certain knife technique where you can take the whole bulb of the garlic, pierce it with the knife in just the right spot, twist your wrist just so, and the clove jumps right out, already peeled. My husband can also open a beer bottle with any item that he has on him. We had a pomegranate tree in our yard, and we loved the seeds of the fruit, but they are such a hassle to harvest. We tried cutting the pomegranate in half and hitting it with a wooden spoon upside down. I think Bobby Flay taught us that one.

The diet and exercise industry is built on hacks. So many people hawking and selling a new idea or method to lose weight, to get in shape without having to put in all the work. Hacks are the lifeblood of the diet and exercise industry and I have fallen for many of them. I get it.

Hacks are really popular and sought after for things that are hard to do, things that may take longer than we are willing to wait, or when it just seems like there should be an easier way. As humans, and especially as Americans, we want an easier, faster, less messy way. Hacks also help us do something that is a major priority or critical, but we don't have all the tools we need to do the job, like opening a bottle of wine or beer on the fly. One day my friend and I went to the beach. We called each other on a beautiful, sunny Saturday and made a last-minute decision to pack a cooler, throw our beach chairs in the car, and drive an hour to meet up. We got settled in our chairs and went to pop open these nice cold beers that we had packed and realized that neither one of us had brought a bottle opener. At first, we despaired, but then I said, "I know we can do this. If my husband were here, he would pop this bottle off the arm of the beach chair." So we tried that without success. But we didn't give up, and we ultimately opened the bottles with our car keys. It worked! We were excited and proud of ourselves.

Hacks are a lot of fun and I'm sure you have some favorites. Perhaps they're related to cooking or drinking, like mine seem to be, or diet and exercise, tools, working out, building something at home, or a construction project.

Unfortunately, there is no hack to leadership. There is no hack, no shortcut, no easy way to become an effective leader. But don't despair. If you've read these lessons, you have the tools. You have practical examples, you have guardrails. You've had your own time in the seat. You can do this. I know you can.

Maybe you're thinking, "You know what, I don't have time to do the hard work. I've got to get this leadership thing figured out or I'm going to be in real trouble at my job."

"I'm going to quit, or I'm just going to give up trying to be a good leader."

"I don't have time to put in this work. I need something that's going to help me right now, tomorrow, to figure this out so I can snap my fingers and be a good leader."

I understand. I know exactly where you're coming from, because I've been there, and I get it.

A couple of years ago, during the Q&A portion of a leadership workshop I hosted, a man raised his hand and asked me a question. He was very sincere and solemn.

"What do you do if you're burned out? What if you're tired of leadership?"

It was a great question and one I wasn't expecting. I thought he was going to ask me something about the material I had presented. I had just spent two hours on the four anchors of *Here to LEAD*, but he was struggling and exhausted and wondering if he wanted to keep doing any of this leadership work. I understood. He was at that leadership conference searching for answers to help him figure out what to do next.

The room full of strangers looked at me silently, waiting expectantly for my words of wisdom and insight, and I'm sure there were other people like him in that room at the time who were frustrated and burned out as well. I knew where he was coming from. I'd been there before. I'd been in a leadership position that is what we traditionally call middle management. You're stuck between a staff that you're trying to manage and motivate and corral, and a senior leadership team who has you running in too many directions putting out fires, and may not even be good leaders themselves, but you report to them. They're driving the organization. So you're stuck in this layer between staff and senior leadership, and this can be a really tough place to be. You want to be a good leader so badly, but you're left drained at the end of the day, feel out of control of your day and your time. You feel out of control of your leadership. I believe the person who asked that question was frustrated because he was probably experiencing some of these things at work, but he was also frustrated because he wasn't sure <u>how</u> to bring his leadership to life on a daily basis. He wasn't seeing the results he desired. Of course, that is frustrating. It is. I get it.

I answered his question with what I truly believe—that authentic leadership is the most critical skill that will allow us to Execute Strategy, Advance Change, and Drive Results. And it is the practical insight, the exercises and the tools that accompany these four anchors that will transform your leadership from a static idea on paper, to life. It will transform your leadership from frustration on a daily basis, from burnout, from wanting to give up and throw in the towel and call it quits, to actually feeling in control of your leadership, in control of your career, in control of your time and your staff and your team and the output that you're providing your organization.

Leadership is an art and like most artists, our craft is a life-long study of trying different techniques that evolve with our experience, our situations and our culture. What works today may not work tomorrow. But the important thing is that we have tools, resources and examples to access when we need them.

These four anchors, the insight, the exercises, the tools, the guardrails, the time in the seat, are the things that will transform your leadership. These are the things that will lead you from frustration to success, from discontent to satisfaction.

 Frustration, burnout, exhaustion and wanting to walk away from being a leader is a direct result of trying to keep our leadership in the fancy living room.

So often, we spend time, money, education and our careers investing in and building this beautiful shrine to leadership, like a lot of people do in their homes when they have a fancy living room or a fancy den that no one is allowed in because they need to keep it in pristine condition all the time. But living rooms are meant to be lived in, right? They are meant to be used. We spend all this money to buy houses and to decorate them and buy all these things that we want to surround ourselves with because we want to live there. We want to experience it. Leadership is the same way.

Leadership is meant to be used. Leadership is meant to be lived in. It doesn't do anyone any good to have your leadership look good on paper, or to sit in your office all day and avoid the hard conversations and the tough decisions, and not know what to do or how to do it. This situation does not benefit anyone. Avoid the fate of the fancy living room.

Instead of looking for the quick answer, the silver bullet, the magic pill, the life hack—embrace the practical, the uncomplicated, the simple, yet hard work, to bring your leadership to life on a daily basis.

It is hard. It is work. But it is worth it.

LEAD. IT'S WHAT YOU'RE HERE FOR.

ACKNOWLEDGMENTS

Occasionally people will ask my husband, Craig, how long it took him to finish a particular painting. He always answers with a smile, "A lifetime," or "About twenty-five years." Of course, the time it took him in the studio, drawing in pencil, creating his value sketch and finally applying the paint, probably took him somewhere between four and fourteen hours, depending on the size and complexity. When Craig answers like this, he is referring to the knowledge and skill he has developed over many years of devotion and dedication to his craft. I could respond the same way when asked about writing this book. Just like becoming a good artist, becoming an effective leader happens when you consistently devote time and study to practice your craft.

My career has been marked with long hours and sleepless nights, stress and insecurities, the constant wondering if I'm making the right decisions or whether or not my career will amount to anything, and most importantly, if I will become a good leader. It has also been full of motivation, ambition, drive and a passionate desire to be successful. To make something better than it was before I arrived. And to do it all with integrity, honesty and sincerity.

I am grateful and thankful for each and every person who has given me the job or let me lead or has worked alongside me, encouraged me and been my friend. Every single position, company and boss with whom I've had the honor and privilege of working, has deposited things in me that have lasted a lifetime. I am the completed demonstration or painting of many artists.

From my dad to my field hockey coach to my pastor, thank you all for pouring into the young version of me your time, your passion and your example of leadership. For every leader, CEO and colleague who has allowed me to develop and learn and grow, thank you for the opportunities, the lessons and for challenging me to do better.

To God be the glory. His unmerited grace and favor in my life has made all the difference, and I am humbled and full of gratitude. The support and love of my husband, my parents and my entire tribe of family and friends sustains me through it all. Thank you.

CPSIA information can be obtained
at www.ICGtesting.com
Printed in the USA
BVHW071037040922
646185BV00002B/13